Southern Literary Studies
Louis D. Rubin, Jr., Editor

A Band of Prophets

From left: Robert Penn Warren, Walter Sullivan, Andrew Lytle, Lyle Lanier, William C. Havard, Cleanth Brooks at the 1980 symposium in honor of the fiftieth year of *I'll Take My Stand*.

Photograph by Jeff T. Carr, Vanderbilt News Service.

A Band of Prophets

The Vanderbilt Agrarians After Fifty Years

Edited, with an Introduction, by
William C. Havard and Walter Sullivan

Louisiana State University Press
Baton Rouge and London

Copyright © 1982 by Louisiana State University Press
All rights reserved
Manufactured in the United States of America

Designer: Joanna Hill
Typeface: Palatino
Typesetter: G&S Typesetters, Inc.
Printer and binder: Thomson-Shore, Inc.

Library of Congress Cataloging in Publication Data
Main entry under title:

A Band of prophets.

(Southern literary studies)
Contents: The South of the Agrarians / Charles P. Roland—For Dixieland /
John Shelton Reed—The southern republic of letters and I'll take my stand /
Lewis P. Simpson—[etc.]
1. I'll take my stand—Addresses, essays, lectures. 2. Southern States—
Civilization—Addresses, essays, lectures. I. Havard, William C. II. Sullivan,
Walter, 1924– . III. Series.
F209.I3732   975   81-19371
ISBN 0-8071-1001-9   AACR2

Contents

Acknowledgments

More people than we can list here helped to organize our commemoration of the fiftieth anniversary of *I'll Take My Stand*. We thank them all, and we are particularly grateful to the following.

Alexander Heard, chancellor of Vanderbilt, and V. Jacque Voegeli, dean of the College of Arts and Sciences at Vanderbilt, both of whom enthusiastically endorsed the idea of the Agrarian celebration from its inception, both of whom furnished financial support, and both of whom participated in the program.

The Special Projects Division of the National Endowment for the Humanities, which provided financial support for the symposium, and Mr. B. J. Stiles and Ms. Linda Moore of the National Endowment for the Humanities. Mr. Stiles brought greetings from the Endowment, and both he and Ms. Moore helped in planning the symposium.

Mr. Brainard Cheney, Ms. Katheryn C. Culbertson, Mrs. Sarah M. Howell, Mr. Murray Hudson, and Professor William H. Race, who served as an advisory committee to the directors of the conference. Their good counsel made our job easier.

Professors Melvin Bradford, Louise Cowan, and Virginia Rock, whose responses to the papers shed much light on the subjects under discussion. We deeply regret that it was not possible to include their responses in this volume.

Professor of English and Vice Chancellor Emeritus Rob Roy Purdy, who presided at the closing session, and President Emmett Fields whose gracious remarks concluded the conference.

Professors Paul Conkin, Herschel Gower, George Graham, William H. Race, and H. L. Weatherby, who led discussion sessions following the presentations of the papers.

Jeff R. Carr, vice president for university relations and general counsel and secretary of the university, Ms. Sharon S. Smith of the Vanderbilt news bureau, Ms. Sue Atkins and Ms. Julie Cruse of Holder Kennedy Public Relations, all of whom helped publicize the symposium. Mrs. Molly Howell Dohrman of WPLN Radio, whose taped program about the Agrarians has become a part of the Fugitive-Agrarian archives. Mrs. Marice M. Wolfe, head of special collections at the Vanderbilt Library, who furnished photographs of the Agrarians and the title page of the first edition of *I'll Take My Stand* which were used in the symposium programs. Mrs. Mary Egerton Higgs, who designed the programs. Mr. Dan Brown, who assisted the directors before, during, and after the conference. Miss Sydney Anderson, who, at the time of the symposium, wrote a special section about the Agrarians for the Vanderbilt *Hustler*.

Ernest Q. Campbell, dean of the Vanderbilt Graduate School, who provided financial assistance for the preparation of the manuscript.

Mrs. Emmett Fields, who extended her generous hospitality to the participants and guests during the conference.

William C. Havard
Walter Sullivan

A Band of Prophets

William C. Havard
and Walter Sullivan

Introduction

In November, 1930, Harper and Brothers, as the publishing firm was then known, brought out a book that at first sight was hardly extraordinary. Although it quickly became controversial and remains so to this day, it was destined eventually to attain the status of a classic because its seemingly topical message (widely regarded initially as anachronistic or reactionary) has commanded more and more credence with the passage of time. Its main title—*I'll Take My Stand*—was a source of contention among the contributors as the plans for the volume materialized, and proved to be a bait to which critics and social commentators rose *en masse* when the book became available for review. The subtitle, *The South and the Agrarian Tradition*, did nothing to lessen the provocation, and may have contributed to some of the naïve misreadings of the book by those both in the North and South who saw it as nothing more than a call to return to a literal agricultural economy, and preferably an agrarian culture that would be as close an approximation as possible to the social and political configurations of the antebellum South. The label "Southern Manifesto" was attached to the contents by friend and foe alike.

The author lines on the cover and title page carried only the attribution, "By Twelve Southerners," although the later paperback editions were to include the names of the "twelve" in alphabetical order on the cover. No editor was listed, and only the introductory "Statement of Principles," by John Crowe Ransom, and the fact that Ransom's essay "Reconstructed but Unregenerate" (actually a composite of two earlier pieces in the *Sewanee Review* and *Harper's*) was the lead article in the book provided clues to a putative intellectual leader among the authors. But in the introduction Ransom was at pains to point out that, while the writers were all southerners, well acquainted with one another, and of similar tastes, perhaps only at the point of publication were they aware of being a group. He went on to note that conversation and correspondence over the years indicated many convictions in common among the participants, but apart from background and consultation no further collaboration was involved; each author was solely responsible for his own article, and only through the good fortune of some deeper agreement was the book expected to achieve its unity. After the affair was well underway it was decided that the shared convictions of the essayists should be set forth in the opening statement of principles to which all contributors then subscribed. In the most succinct expression of the underlying symbolic unity on which the loosely cooperative activity leading to the book (and for that matter to the subsequent activities of the Agrarians), Ransom indicated that "all tend to support a Southern way of life against what may be called the American or prevailing way; and all as much as agree that the best terms in which to present the distinction are contained in the phrase, Agrarian *versus* Industrial."

Whatever deeply rooted loyalties and philosophical convictions may have bound the group into a small literary community, the diversity among the individuals composing it was equally apparent. And this diversity was reflected in the varieties of literary genre and style, as well as in the philosophical and ideological ranges represented in *I'll Take My Stand*. In addition to Ransom, three other contributors—Donald Davidson, Allen Tate, and Robert Penn Warren—had earlier been central figures in that remarkable literary group of the early 1920s known as the Vanderbilt Fugitives and as organizers and publishers of the poetry magazine *The Fugitive* (1922–1925). And though Tate and Warren, who had been co-opted into the Fugitive society as precocious undergraduates, had left Vanderbilt by the time the Agrarian movement was fully "organized" (Tate to follow his early literary career in New York and Paris, and Warren to pursue his studies as a Rhodes Scholar at Oxford), the Agrarians were in many respects a translation of the Fugitives into a new, and more public, form of activity. As faculty members in the English Department at Vanderbilt throughout the Fugitive and Agrarian periods, Davidson and Ransom were the on-site stimulators of much of the correspondence and conversation that led to the idea of the book. Tate, who had an uncanny capacity for managing ventures at great distances from the center of events, was heavily engaged in the later aspects of the project, especially the arrangements for publication. Warren was not as much involved as the others, although he and Tate joined in opposition to the title, and he ended up accepting the responsibility for what was probably the most difficult essay in the book—"The Briar Patch"—which deals with the need to make a place for the Negro in the South.

In addition to this core group who were both Fugitives and Agrarians, several other members of the Vanderbilt faculty were at the center of the discussions leading to the eventual decision to assemble and publish the sweeping manifesto. They included Lyle Lanier, a member of the psychology department and an early student of the psychology of race, whose essay "A Critique of the Philosophy of Progress" continues to be one of the best critical analyses of the peculiarly American version of the ideology of progress; Herman Clarence Nixon, a mildly populistic political scientist whose essay on the southern economy outlines the only practical program for Agrarian reform to be found in the book; Frank L. Owsley, an eminent American historian and framer of the yeoman farmer theme in southern historiography; and John Donald Wade, biographer, essayist, and preceptor at large in the art of gracious living in one's place of origin. Although not teaching at Vanderbilt, Andrew Lytle had been a student at the university in the 1920s, and in seeking to combine farming with a literary career during the early years of the Depression was so close an associate of the group that he has to be regarded as a member of the inner circle of Agrarians. His hyperbolic plea on behalf of the simple rural life in "The Hind Tit" is cast in the light fictional mold of the naturally gifted storyteller.

Other contributors were brought in from a greater or lesser distance in terms of background, geography, or occupation. Two of them, Stark Young (the oldest contributor at forty-nine) and John Gould Fletcher, were already figures of considerable distinction in the literary world and had their connection through personal and professional relations with the Vanderbilt core. Young was from Mississippi and Fletcher from Arkansas; the former was best known in the twenties and early thirties as a drama critic for several national papers and magazines, and the latter, who lived in England for many years, had a substantial reputation as a widely published poet in the imagist vein. Although Henry Blue Kline was a native Tennessean and even, in Virginia Rock's phrase, "of a later generation of Vanderbilt students," his career in journalism and public service removed him somewhat from the resident core, with whom, how-

ever, he was in fairly close touch (mainly by correspondence) during the planning of *I'll Take My Stand*.

In addition to being southerners, then, the contributors
had in common a stringent critical attitude toward the trend
in American society away from humane values in the direction of a technocratic, urban-industrial society organized on
a mass basis around a cash nexus, producer-consumer relation. Having explored, in the Fugitive phase, some of the
conditions that made possible an environment in which the
arts could flourish, they shared the need to examine those
positive economic, social, and religious values out of which
the good life and its profound expression in art was possible. They also had in common a great measure of talent,
which naturally varied among the individuals, both in degree and in the objectives toward which it was directed. As
a relatively youthful group (four were in their twenties, the
average age was about thirty-five, and only one was beyond
the mid-forties) they also had the will to try to affect the
pace and direction of historic change which, despite many
charges against them to the contrary, they saw as a continuing part of man's finite existence.

The diversity of the group contributed much to the way
their deeper unity was manifested. They ranged in pragmatic political and social orientation from traditional, pater-
nalistic conservatives through the advocates of the yeoman
middle class as the necessary solid base of a well-ordered
society, to those who viewed the populist cause with sympathy and were later proponents of many of the New Deal
programs. Although a majority were literary in their voca-
tions, the group included some with a bent for formal economic and social analysis and public administration, and all
of them had strong interests in and considerable capacities
for using historical and philosophical, as well as literary,
means of making human experience coherent. The essays

thus range from those reflecting closely reasoned logical argument through virtually all other rhetorical modes of persuasion and varieties of creative literary expression. Some essays appeal to the sentiments, others to reason in both the instrumental and the noetic senses of the term; some are hortatory, while others use the gentler appeal of exemplification. Some are harshly critical while others use criticism only as an entry into the affirmations of traditional principles. Most combine several types of argumentation to validate their central theses. Running through the entire book are traces of tragedy, melodrama, and comedy, cast in poetic, fictional, dramatic, historical, and philosophic language. The persisting appeal of the social and political message of the book and the sustained quality of the varied literary styles of the authors in combination make *I'll Take My Stand* a work that has maintained its contemporaneity for more than fifty years.

Ironically, not many critics accepted the book as a relevant statement when it was published. Its themes were distorted by romantic southerners who longed for a restoration of plantation life; by well known northern progressives who distrusted anything southern; and by southern journalists and intellectuals who had embraced the myth of progress and the materialistic goals of the "New South." And although it never sold very well and was either limitedly available or out of print altogether after a relatively short time, it has continuously been a standard object of discussion in academic and literary circles since the early 1930s. As Allen Tate noted, it was treated in every conceivable way, but it was never ignored.

One of the persisting criticisms of the Agrarians was that they constructed a literary image of an ideal society but failed to address the issue of bringing such a community into pragmatic existence. The contributors themselves differed on this question. In the period immediately following the appearance of *I'll Take My Stand* Ransom was actively involved in pressing for action. He lectured widely and debated some prominent critics of the book, undertook the study of economics and planned and wrote a draft treatise on the subject from the Agrarian perspective. He and several other central figures in the group also published a number of critical essays on economic and political questions in the *American Review* and similar periodicals. In the later 1930s Tate and Herbert Agar coedited a volume of essays entitled *Who Owns America?*, which was considered in some ways a sequel to the Agrarian Manifesto. Most of the original Agrarians were contributors, and they were joined by a group of English Distributists, including Hilaire Belloc, who was the initiator of that movement. By that time, however, the activist imperative had declined among the Agrarians. Most of them had returned almost entirely to their literary and academic preoccupations. Only Nixon and Kline were participants in both official and voluntary capacities in a number of social and economic reform programs; only Davidson never abandoned the effort to persuade his colleagues to plan and implement a practical agrarian program.

In the years following the publication of *I'll Take My Stand*, many of the contributors gained substantial literary reputation, and in the nation as a whole, profound social and political changes were underway. Tate, Ransom, Davidson, Warren, and Lytle were major figures in the Southern Literary Renascence. The New Deal and, later, the economic development of the South during and after World War II moved the region steadily toward an industrial, urban configuration. And though the practical warnings of the Agrarians were seemingly ignored by southerners, as they had earlier been scorned by commentators outside the region, the universally acknowledged achievement of the writers of the Southern Renascence imposed on their critics an obligation to make a new and serious examination of the southern heritage. In 1956 a Fugitive reunion was held in Nashville, and one of the sessions was devoted to a discussion of the Agrarian experience. It was generally agreed (with one or two of those present dissenting) that the two endeavors really were phases of a single movement, the one growing naturally out of the other, and that the artistic concerns of the Fugitives could not be separated from the social and political concerns of the Agrarians.

Inasmuch as *I'll Take My Stand* had continued to be read and discussed as part of the revival (or more accurately, the *emergence*) of southern letters, Harper reissued it as a Torchbook paperback in 1962, with an introduction by Louis Rubin and a set of brief biographical essays by Virginia Rock. Fifteen years later the LSU Press acquired publication rights and included the book in its Library of Southern Civilization. The events of the 1960s and 1970s— foreign and domestic policy failures, environmental depredation, stagflation, urban decay, loss of confidence in institutions, (and many other sources of President Carter's perception of a national "malaise")—seemed strikingly to fulfill the prediction made by the Agrarians in the 1930s. And most of the harbingers of change in the direction of the postindustrial society seemed to be echoing the half-century-old calls of the Agrarians for an economy and society organized on a human scale, one that permits more individual, family, and community control over personal and social destinies than does the centralized industrial state, and one that reflects more concern with spiritual and humane values than is fostered by the scientistic-technocratic-industrial mode of existence.

By the fiftieth anniversary of its publication *I'll Take My Stand* had come full circle. Although neither the book nor its vision of a proper order of man and society was ever submerged completely, both were now back in full view. And seen in retrospect *I'll Take My Stand* is widely perceived today not as a nostalgic look backward, but as a forward-looking, even prophetic book. It is no longer regarded as a defense of a particular (and highly romanticized) local culture so much as an affirmation of universal values in relation to a political, social, and cultural struggle in which the survival of the religious, aesthetic, and moral foundations of the old European civilization were at stake. It is also more difficult now to accept the smug assurance of those who interpreted it as a literal call to reify a pastoral dream in the face of its acceptance as a metaphorical way of drawing the contrast between a society organized solely for the purpose of producing and acquiring material goods to satisfy the appetitive instincts and one that might find better means of fulfilling the rational and spiritual, as well as the corporeal, needs of man conceived in a fuller human dimension. Even the concreteness of its southern reference point cannot be so readily turned against it as it was in books published as late as the 1960s, since the South, despite its rapid urban-industrial development, has somehow managed to retain certain qualities and values of a pre-modern or traditional culture (personalism, attachment to extended family and to place, a sense of history and of religious commitment) as possible useful guides to life in the tentative emergence of postindustrialism.

The book in hand, then, is a book celebrating the fiftieth birthday of another book: *I'll Take My Stand: The South and the Agrarian Tradition*, by Twelve Southerners. Like the book it celebrates, this one was conceived in conversation and correspondence among friends, who in this case were concerned about how Vanderbilt University might suitably honor a remarkable association of faculty members and alumni (whose contribution to the university's heritage is incalculable) on the golden anniversary of one of their most important collective achievements. Although the idea that a book might be forthcoming as a product of other activities was expressed at the outset of the discussion, plans centered from the beginning on a public event cast in the form of a symposium on the meaning of *I'll Take My Stand* after fifty years. The sessions were held on October 30, 31, and November 1 on the Vanderbilt campus, and the tightly packed events during the two days from Thursday afternoon through Saturday morning had the dual character of a well-attended conference and a reunion of family and friends. We were fortunate in having the three living Agrarians as participants, and their presence attracted numerous members of their own families as well as relatives of the other contributors, many of their contemporaries, and former and present colleagues and students.

The text which follows consists of revised and edited versions of the six principal papers presented at the first three sessions of the symposium, together with an edited transcript of the Saturday morning panel discussion among the surviving contributors to *I'll Take My Stand*. Although many others who attended the symposium assisted generously in the planning stages and were active participants in the program (as indicated in the acknowledgments), problems of space and the critical judgment that the volume should realize the coherence of a monograph rather than attempt the comprehensiveness of a proceedings persuaded us to pare the contents to its present form.

Collectively, the authors of the papers that constitute the first six chapters, and Cleanth Brooks, who moderated the panel, resemble the contributors to the book they examine here in that they are all southerners save one, and even he has not escaped the charge of being a long-time sympathizer. They, too, are friends and associates who not only share many convictions and values, but who also have a common vocational interest in understanding the history, literature, society, and culture of the South. And like their Fugitive and Agrarian predecessors, they come to their subject from the perspectives of several academic disciplines and a variety of other interests. In one way or another, nearly all of them have been colleagues, students, or successors in various editorial or other capacities of one or more of the Agrarians. If they are, in this sense, direct descendants or even, in one or two instances, members of the outer circle of the Agrarians, and thus natural sympathizers with what *I'll Take My Stand* was all about, they come to the book with a knowledge of its background and of the text itself that would be difficult to duplicate among any other group of individuals, and with a critical scholarly integrity that cannot be compromised.

In extending invitations to the principal participants, the editors suggested the general subjects to be addressed in the papers and by the panelists largely on the basis of the special interests reflected in previously published work, as this was related to our desire to provide a careful examination of the background, meaning, persisting intellectual influence, and contextual implications of the Agrarian effort. But no attempt was made to influence the way in which each contributor handled his subject, which in almost every essay includes some reaffirmations of accepted interpretations, accompanied by some additional insights and, in several of the essays, completely new perspectives or themes.

The first two essays are by a historian and a social scientist: they provide the historical background and cultural context out of which the Agrarians proceeded and to which they added an important self-interpretative theme. Charles Roland gives a panoramic view of the South of the 1920s and its particular relation to the nation at large. He sees the Agrarians as part of the dialectical process involving the consciousness of differences between the southern historical experience and that of the rest of the country, and the repeated cycle of attempted reconciliations and mutual rejections those distinctions evoked. At their entry into this process the Agrarians responded, at first defensively, but in their larger vision positively, to a sustained cultural, political, and economic attack on the South, and their defense was based on humane values derived from a traditional religious and moral view of the nature of man in the face of the modern scientific (or naturalistic) conception of human nature.

John Shelton Reed follows with an analysis of the way in which the Agrarians heightened perceptions of those cultural differences that are clearly there, and which Reed himself had earlier affirmed as continuing even in the flux of recent social change in the South. He examines the way in which the contributors to *I'll Take My Stand* found in a refurbished southern myth and tradition a satisfactory response to the questions of human dignity and self-respect which they were concerned to defend against the cultural, economic, and political assaults on them from outside the region. He goes beyond this affirming analysis, however, and brings established theoretical categories applicable to the development of national consciousness among certain types of intellectuals to throw additional light, at least tentatively, on southern sectionalism and cultural nationalism. And he extends this perception by holding that, as artists, the Agrarians spoke to issues more enduring than the ethnic or regional conflicts that were the immediate occasion for their tracts or manifesto.

The next two essays turn to the meaning of *I'll Take My Stand* as literature in relation to the broader and more ancient European culture and its newer but no less historically rooted place in a Southern Republic of Letters.

Lewis Simpson's essay, "The Southern Republic of Letters and *I'll Take My Stand*," is an extension of the philosophical theme he has been developing in recent studies of the literary vocation in America. Since the eighteenth century the secularized mind of literature and science (now conflated into "science") has become the source of meaning and order in human affairs and the motive force of history, displacing the ritualized, sacramental order characteristic of traditional societies. In an artist's revolt against this main tendency of modernity the Agrarians aimed at restoring a world of myth and tradition as embodied in Tate's conception of an agrarian metaphor that had its true origin in the old European society. Simpson thus confirms, in a much broader and deeper philosophical interpretation of the movement of history, the workings of the literary mind, and the symbolization of man's life in society, the old thesis that the Southern Renascence resulted from the awareness of those who comprised a Southern Republic of Letters that society as a unity of mind, body, spirit, and community was threatened with extinction by the "dissociation of sensibility" (T. S. Eliot's phrase) characteristic of modernity.

In "Spokesman and Seer" Robert Heilman addresses in a subtly evocative way the question of the civilizational values inherent in the literary arts used by the Agrarians to make their case. In doing so he employs his own fine blend of personal experience in conjunction with a full awareness of how that experience is writ large in the major literary traditions in England and on the continent. The Agrarians, especially Ransom and Tate, were anxious to establish this tradition as an antecedent connection with the South. A well-established scholar in the theory of literary genre, Heilman is adept in fixing the specifics and calculating the effect of the literary variety in the Agrarian essays. And his own rhetorical skill is reflected in the way he steadily expands his generously illustrated argument to show how the Agrarians moved from their actions as spokesmen in defense of a specific tradition to the status of seers who perceive and articulate the universality of meaning in the particular.

The two final papers return to the questions about the Agrarians as men of letters. In his eclectical essay, "Agrarianism, Criticism, and the Academy," George Core exposes the difficulties encountered by the inner circle of Agrarians in their efforts to place the pursuit of the literary arts at the forefront of their activities. His comments on the breadth of their writing, whether considered individually or collectively, reveals much about the unifying, holistic nature of their work. First engaged almost exclusively with poetry, they branched into every area of literature—fiction, history, biography, social commentary, philosophy, editing, and criticism. Through the last of these they returned to, and in some ways captured, the academy, and through it they disseminated widely their conceptions of literature and the cultural foundations of society. Thus they affirmed the unity of the literary arts with the whole range of human experience, and exemplified in their own works the imaginative synthesis they sought to realize in the individual and society in the face of the disintegrative tendencies of modernity.

After wryly observing at the outset of his paper on the literary tradition and *I'll Take My Stand* that he doesn't know what he will have to say that he has not already said (and probably better) in writing repeatedly about the Agrarians over a twenty-five-year period, Louis Rubin goes on to reinforce his persistent thesis that the importance of the book is primarily as a literary work, and its survival is due largely to its literary quality. He then provides not only a critical analysis of the literary mode (the "foreground") of the book, but a cogent exposition, with appropriate excerpts of both concrete metaphorical and direct expressions of the English and American literary tradition to which it is most closely related (its "literary background"). In this apposite exegesis Rubin succeeds in refuting his own contention about having nothing new to say on the subject.

The Saturday morning (November 1, 1980) session was the conclusion of the Agrarian Symposium and it is appropriate, we think, that the edited transcript of that session should conclude this book. The three contributors to *I'll Take My Stand* were convened as a panel under the mediating hand of Cleanth Brooks. The subject addressed by Messrs. Lanier, Lytle, and Warren was "The Agrarian-Industrial Metaphor: Culture, Economics, and Society in a Technological Age," but attention to the general theme, "*I'll Take My Stand*: A Fiftieth Anniversary Retrospective by Three of the Authors," was probably the larger expectation in the minds of most of those present, and these expectations were not disappointed. In speaking to the formal topic (which the panelists did in a most contemporary manner) the hovering presence of what was said fifty years before was always felt and often spoken to directly or referred to allusively.

What came through most clearly in the oral exchange, and is, we think, well preserved in the transcribed version, was the sustained vigor with which the participants joined the issues as though the fifty years that had elapsed were no more than that number of months or even days. The marks of easily renewed friendship and the potent memories of commitment to a common cause are revealed as fully to the reader as they were to the live audience, although some of the by-play, expressions, and intonations obviously cannot be captured in print.

The panelists strongly reaffirmed the justice of their criticism first enunciated in 1930 of the dehumanizing perils of a headlong rush into the urban-industrial society. They argued that the events of recent years not only proved their case but demonstrated how much their critique erred on the side of restraint. They also agreed that they may have fallen short in their stress on developing individual, family, community, and religious values in opposition to those emerging from a technological, materialistic, mass-organizational society. And in speaking once again to the nature of the problems that beset such a society, they returned to the quest for understanding man in the wholeness of his being: his search for a coherent identity, his individuality and its social supports in family and community, his place in nature. More than that, the panelists spoke of those rational and spiritual qualities that cause man to search for moral truth and to reach toward transcendence, and of his needs to express himself through myth, art, and religion.

Finally, one notes how the rhetorical styles of the panelists vary and yet complement each other, again recalling the characteristic unity in diversity of *I'll Take My Stand*. After Brooks frames the questions, Lanier moves in with a fine analytical perspective, amplified by current explanatory theories to which the others can relate. Lytle, who remains the storyteller *par excellence*, develops his themes as parables that pique the imagination and turn from near absurdity into subtly finished moral truths. And Warren, the poet-philosopher, is always economical with words, allusive, and metaphorical, while capping his remarks with just the right aphoristic generalization, with the tag sometimes quietly repeated, as though to himself, for rhythmic poetic emphasis.

We repeat that this is a book about another book that spoke persuasively and generally to the social conditions under which life in human terms could be most fully realized, and did so in language that reflects the full range of

rational discourse embodied in the historical, philosophical, and literary arts. It is fitting that it should conclude with
the discussion by some of the original contributors of the
persisting human issues as they confront us today; and it is
not surprising that their discourse should reflect the abid-
ing force of their critical intelligence expressed in characteristic literary forms.

Charles P. Roland

The South of the Agrarians

The South of the 1920s, like the South at any other point in its long history, was something of an enigma. It was in the United States and of the United States, yet it was distinct from the rest of the United States. As late as 1941 Wilbur J. Cash would say the South was not quite a nation within a nation, but that it was the next thing to it.

Southerners did not have to be taught from books that the South's history was different from that of the nation as a whole. Everybody knew, however imperfectly, that the South had once been a Cotton Kingdom with plantations worked by black slaves; that it had attempted to become an independent nation, only to be defeated in war and forced to remain within the Union; that the slaves had been freed in the course of the struggle and then had been granted citizenship, both against the will of southern whites; that the South was occupied by federal armies and subjected to the authority of Carpetbaggers, Scalawags, and ex-slaves; and that this regime had been overthrown by southern white violence and fealty to the Democratic party.

The actual history of these events was often twisted in the southern mind, exaggerated by time and telling, by prejudice and pride. The legendary Old South became an idyllic land of kind and gracious masters and obedient and mistreatment. Strong ties of affection developed among countless individual whites and blacks. But all classes of whites agreed that the blacks must "stay in their places." So apparently immutable was this determination that Ulrich B. Phillips called it the "Central Theme" of southern history.

The South was traditionally the poor cousin of the affluent American society. Its economy had always been predominantly agricultural; at the time of the Civil War the eleven Confederate states produced less than 10 percent of the nation's manufactured wares as measured by sale value. In spite of great efforts after the war to industrialize itself, the South in the early decades of the twentieth century was still largely agricultural. It still depended heavily on its historic crop—cotton. Indeed, in some ways cotton dominated the South more in the 1920s than it had on the eve of the Civil War. There were now four times as many acres in cotton as in the 1850s. The regional economy was essentially colonial. Southerners sold their farm produce and natural resources such as timber and oil to feed the national industrial machine, at the same time importing from the North the bulk of their manufactured goods such as plows, harvesters, and automobiles. Estimates in 1919 indicated that southern per capita income was 40 percent below the national average. The disparity between the southern income and that of the wealthier states of the Northeast, Midwest, or Pacific Coast was much wider. A survey taken in the late 1930s caused President Franklin D. Roosevelt to call the South the nation's "No. 1 economic problem."

Southern politics served to protect the region's traditional interests and prejudices within the national political framework. Having emerged from Reconstruction through what may be termed paramilitary means under the leadership of former Confederate officers, the southern voters long gave these men their full allegiance at the polls. Election to southern office in the late nineteenth century without the badge of honor of a Confederate battle wound was almost unheard of. When General Francis T. Nicholls of Louisiana was running for the governorship of that state, minus an arm and foot lost in the war, he was introduced to audiences with the words: "I present to you what is left of General Nicholls." A South Carolinian writing in the 1930s remembered United States Senator Wade Hampton, a former Confederate hero, as "the limping apotheosis of the Lost Cause."

To the southern people such men were known as "The Redeemers" because they had saved the South from its alleged tormentors. To less sympathetic, outside observers they were "The Bourbons," who, like the restored royal family of France, had neither forgotten anything of the ancient regime nor learned anything from the Revolution. Under whatever title, they were conservative in their political, social, and economic views. Their major commitments to the voters were to keep whites in control of affairs and to practice competence, honesty, and frugality in running their administrations. To the first of these commitments they were faithful; to the rest of them their devotion was more erratic.

An agrarian or small-farmer revolt against the Redeemers (or Bourbons, if you please) occurred near the end of the century. Led by such fiery orators as Tom Watson of Georgia and Pitchfork Ben Tillman of South Carolina, the small farmers of the South gained a more influential voice in regional politics. Early in the twentieth century the reform movement known as progressivism, championed largely by the middle classes, took control of most southern state administrations and sent many of their leaders to Congress. By 1920, southern politics had come to represent a blend of all three of these forces.

But this diversity was overshadowed by a stronger unity. Whether Bourbon, Agrarian, or Progressive, the vast majority of voting southerners were Democrats, thus giving the region the name "the Solid South." Many voters became known as "Yellow Dog Democrats" because they were said to have declared they would support a yellow dog for office rather than a Republican. To add spice to political life, and perhaps to give emphasis by humorous distortion, the story was sometimes told of such a Democrat who on one occasion was so displeased with his party's candidate that he voted for the Republican opponent. Reminded of his vow, he admitted having made it. "But," he explained, "the Democrats didn't run a yellow dog this time, and lower than that I will not go." The Democratic primaries, almost everywhere "lily white" (closed to blacks), were in effect the final elections. Frequently the Republicans declined even to put up candidates. The fundamental characteristics of southern politics were Democratic hegemony and white supremacy.

To nonsoutherners the South was a backward country area relieved here and there by the charm of a Charleston, a Mobile, or a Savannah, or of a white-columned, rural antebellum plantation mansion. The old abolitionist fantasy of dividing white southerners into two classes only—the fabulously rich and powerful lords of manors and the squalid and torpid poor whites—still had a strong influence on popular thought. The region was, in fact, the most rural part of twentieth-century America. Three out of four southerners in 1920 were classified by the federal census as being rural. Approximately half the total population made their livings as farmers, neither rich nor poor in the traditional planter or poor-white sense. The bulk of the non-farming population lived in the thousands of towns and villages that dotted the countryside. Only about 10 percent of the region's inhabitants lived in cities of 100,000 or more population. Finally, the cities themselves were more or less large country towns because they were relatively small (Atlanta 200,000, for example), and because of the strong ties of blood and culture existing between the city folk and their country kin.

Thus, despite the inroads of industrialism and urbanism, the South of the 1920s preserved in great measure the conventions and flavor of the old rural life. Along with the newfangled nightclubbing and such immensely popular spectator sports as college football, many of the more traditional diversions remained, including horsemanship and hunting and fishing. Because of the mildness of the climate, the great expanses of open fields and woods, and the countless natural streams and lakes, the South probably had more hunters and fishers than any other population of comparable numbers in the world.

The core of southern society was the family, and the South's failure to receive any significant proportion of the European immigrants who entered the United States in the nineteenth century and early twentieth century gave the entire southern population a family-like homogeneity. Actual blood ties were extraordinarily strong; outsiders said any two southerners who got together would ultimately discover they were cousins. Family reunions and community homecomings were memorable social occasions, sometimes attracting stray kinfolk from as far away as Chicago or Los Angeles. Home cooking was a source of immense family pride, featuring dishes made from the secret recipes of Aunt Nancy or Aunt Millie, ladies who, at least in some instances, were spinster casualties of the Civil War. Seasoning the food was usually done by the pinch and taste method. The hot biscuit, cornbread, and fried chicken line was as authentic a regional boundary as the Mason-Dixon line.

Though the South was the stronghold of the Prohibition movement, and the southern churches inveighed also against dancing, card-playing, and what was euphemistically called "petting," the region was known as well for its hard drinking and other weaknesses of the flesh. In New Orleans it had a community celebrated far and wide for its love of pleasure—a city of sin at the end of the big river. Someone has remarked that New Orleans was a safety valve for a people reared in a strict Calvinistic tradition; that the city provided them an opportunity for escaping their inhibitions and discharging their emotions, even if frequently it was done by surrogate. Cash said the South offered the world's greatest paradox of hedonism in the midst of puritanism.

Drawing upon the aristocratic, plantation ideal, southerners gave allegiance to the cult of manners, for they looked upon form as being indivisible from function or substance. The words *chivalry* and *chivalric*, free of any sense of derision, were not at all uncommon on the southern tongue. As late as the mid-1930s in the city of Nashville (or in other southern cities) one might see a half-dozen men rise simultaneously to offer a woman a seat on a crowded trolley. Even the poorest and least-educated southerner, said Cash, deported himself with a certain level-eyed courtesy and ease of bearing derived from the customs of the gentry. Hand in hand with the cult of manners went a cult of violence. Being a population of hunters, and perhaps also because they were votaries of a strong military tradition, almost all southerners owned firearms. Southerners more than others were prone to resort to trial by combat in settling personal disputes. The region steadily held the nation's highest homicide rates. The emphasis on manners coupled with that on violence gave rise to the saying that a southerner would remain polite until he was angry enough to kill.

Accompanying and reinforcing the economic, political, and social factors of southern distinctiveness was a set of equally distinguishing cultural characteristics. Among these, no force was stronger than that of religion in developing and sustaining a southern ethos. Church membership was more common in the South than elsewhere, and most southerners who were not on the church rolls shared the world view of those who were on the rolls. Overwhelmingly orthodox Protestant, the membership was heavily concentrated in the white and black branches of the southern Baptist and Methodist churches, the southern Presbyterian church, and the Churches of Christ. Many southerners also were attracted to the numerous Pentecostal and Holiness bodies, which were largely of southern origin.

Edwin McNeill Poteat, Jr., said the churches were arranged along class lines, the Episcopalians at the top of the social and economic scale, the Presbyterians in the middle, and the Methodists and Baptists at the bottom. Though he omitted a number of groups and, doubtless intentionally, exaggerated the class thesis for those he listed, his statement was accurate in that southern religion did accommodate itself to social distinctions. There was a saying handed down from the Old South that many roads lead to heaven, but the true southern gentleman would follow the Episcopal route.

The variety of denominations and their class arrangements failed to destroy the region's theological conformity. Regardless of church affiliation, the Word of God as revealed in the Bible continued to provide the masses of the southern population their fundamental philosophy. Southerners accepted scientific technology, but they would not yield the belief that "man holds a position in the universe under divine guidance"; they refused to convert science into a religion. Southern belief in a literal interpretation of the Bible was strong enough to cause many states to enact statutes prohibiting the teaching in state-supported schools of any idea, including Darwin's theory of the evolution of species, that contradicted the literal Genesis account of the creation of man.

An English writer traveling in the South in 1910 observed: "The South is by a long way the most simply and sincerely religious country that I was ever in. . . . It is a country in which religion is a very large factor in life, and God is very real and personal." At mid-century Hodding Carter was still moved to say: "Though the citadels crumble, the South remains the great western-world stronghold of Protestant, fundamentalist Christianity. . . . That thing called the old-time religion is in the blood of most of us, and if it is laughed at, the laughter has an accompaniment of inescapable inner, esoteric warning that the ways of God are not to be mocked by man."

Southern churches were not completely untouched by the winds of liberalism, or modernism, as it was usually called in the South. In public matters the leading denominations supported the aims of the Progressive movement, including such humanitarian measures as the regulation of the working conditions for women and children, the right of laborers to form and join unions, and the entire set of political reforms that were then being heralded as forces for the uplift of society. The churches also sponsored the building of hospitals, schools, orphanages, and homes for the outcast and indigent. Many educated southerners accepted such unorthodox teachings as the Higher Criticism of the Bible and the theory of the evolution of man. The upper economic and social classes tended to substitute for the religious fervor and emotionalism of earlier times a comfortable reconciliation with secular ideas and worldly ways.

But the dominant religious energies of the South were directed to otherworldliness and the salvation of individual souls rather than the reform of society. Southerners were the least utopian of Americans; the teachings of the Social Gospel, popular in other areas, made slow headway in the South. The precepts of southern religion reinforced the lessons of southern history to keep the people from believing in the earthly perfectability of man. Robert Penn Warren remained true to his southern upbringing when he caused the central figure in his novel *All the King's Men* (published in 1945) to say he had thoroughly learned about the sinful nature of mankind in his childhood Sunday school training in Louisiana.

Religious conservatism touched all aspects of life in the South. It kept alive the puritanism that struggled with the natural love of pleasure among the people. It emphasized the vital role of the family in God's plan for society. It strengthened the color line both through its theological explanation of race relations and through the role of the churches, white and black, in observing social convention. Even the region's economic plight was alleged by some to be the result of its religious convictions. "In religion," said Broadus Mitchell, "the past has stretched forth her hand and held us fast. . . . We have remained like Mary enraptured at the Master's feet, and have refused to have a part in the workaday world, or be like Martha, 'anxious about many things.'" One of the most knowledgeable students of the southern mind, C. Vann Woodward, has written that the "exuberant religiosity" of the South persisted powerfully into the twentieth century and was largely responsible for the homogeneity of the people and the readiness with which they responded to common impulses; that, indeed, it explained much of the survival of a distinctive regional culture.

Southern literature also supported and reflected the region's outlook on itself and the rest of the world. Because this topic is to be thoroughly discussed by others in later gatherings of this symposium, I shall not attempt any analysis of it here. Permit me to say simply that the South has traditionally been a highly verbal society. The politicians, preachers, journalists, novelists, and poets of the Old South mobilized the language in defense of slavery and the other activities and ideas that made up the southern "way of life." In the years after the Civil War the most celebrated southern writers, the local colorists, presented a mellow view of the Old South and superimposed upon it the tragic theme of the Lost Cause of the Confederacy. Thomas Nelson Page, quoted earlier in this essay, was perhaps the most popular of this group. Finally, the entire body of southern writers and rhetoricians provided the base for the twentieth-century flowering of southern letters known as the Southern Renascence, a most significant element in which was the Fugitive and Agrarian movement at Vanderbilt University.

The South was never particularly distinguished in the fine arts. Only in its architecture, in the adaptation of European and classical modes to the southern environment, did the Old South demonstrate an outstanding aesthetic quality. The architecture of the post–Civil War South was often imitative and banal. There were, of course, exceptions. A notable one was the work of Neel Reid, an early twentieth-century Atlanta architect, who inspired a revival of the colonial Georgian style tastefully set in the wooded hills on the outskirts of his city.

The most sustained artistic effort to express overtly the region's awareness of its historic distinctiveness occurred in sculpture. The chief activity in this medium during the half-century following the Civil War was the placing of a nondescript Confederate soldier in stone on virtually every courthouse square. Sculpture of genuine merit included the recumbent statue of General Robert E. Lee at Lexington, Virginia, by Edward M. Valentine, the equestrian statue of Lee at Richmond, by Jean Antoine Mercié, and the recumbent statue of General Albert Sidney Johnston at Austin, by Elisabet Ney. In 1923 on the face of Stone Mountain in Georgia, Gutzon Borglum began the colossal figures of Lee, Jefferson Davis, and General Stonewall Jackson, but the work soon halted and would remain unfinished until after World War II.

The most original artistic contribution made by the South was its folk music. Of greatest appeal during the 1920s were the black spirituals, which in turn brought recognition to other forms of Afro-American music and its derivatives, including blues and jazz. The ancestral white folk music, ballads, and white spirituals also remained alive in the rural and mountainous areas of the South, but these styles and their offshoots, hillbilly music and ultimately country music and gospel music, would be slower in claiming the enthusiasm of the American public.

Clearly the South in the 1920s exhibited a great variety of social and cultural traits. The region was not isolated geographically from the rest of the nation. It offered no impenetrable linguistic barrier, though its differences in accent and cadence may have tempted some observers to say of northerners and southerners what Shaw said of Englishmen and Americans: that they were two peoples separated by a common language. The South was not impervious to outside ideas. But as David M. Potter has convincingly explained, the region's long and intimate experience as a rural society had the effect of preserving into the twentieth century strong elements of an older folk culture which tended to offset, even to repudiate, the urban-industrial culture that by now was far advanced in the other major sections of the country. In this folk culture, said Potter, the people retained a more direct and primal relationship with the land, with nature in general, and with one another. Also, one might add, a more direct and primal relationship with God.

But forces had long been at work that threatened the traditional culture of the South and sought to bring the region into the wide channel of national progress. The banner under which these forces marched was that of the New South. A title actually coined by a Union officer during the Civil War, the expression "The New South" was taken over in the 1870s and 1880s by a group of enterprising young southerners who by circumstance and timing were ready to lead an important transition in southern thinking. The most imaginative and most colorful of the group was the Atlanta journalist and raconteur Henry W. Grady.

Grady and his cohorts did not consciously assault the region's culture. These men held a vision of the future in which the virtue and grace of the Old South, now that it was rid of the burden of slavery, would blend with a vigor and industry copied from the victorious North. The New South, as they expressed it, was simply to be the Old South under new conditions. Thus, in the words of a leading present-day student of the movement, Paul M. Gaston, the original New South adherents sought to maintain a "vital nexus" between the modern impulses of material progress and the traditional values of the South. The unanswered question was: "Would the vital nexus hold?"

The New South advocates deplored the economic colonialism of the South, its dependence on the North for manufactured wares and even for many of its items of food. Grady illustrated this dependence with two stories, neither original to him, but both of which he made famous. In one of the stories he described a pre–Civil War Georgia funeral, for which, he said, the hearse, the clothing, and every other commodity had been imported from the North—except the corpse and the hole in the ground. Both of these probably would have been imported, Grady said, if it had been possible to do so. In his other story Grady told of having made two trips, one in a section of Pennsylvania grown rich through the planting of tobacco and another in a section of North Carolina impoverished through the planting of the same kind of crop. The difference was, he explained, that in Pennsylvania tobacco was the money crop of a diversified agriculture while in North Carolina it was grown to the neglect of everything else, thus obliging the farmers to purchase all their necessities from outsiders at premium cost. Grady and his associates urged the South to become prosperous through industrialization and the diversification of agriculture.

The New South spokesmen were convinced by their own rhetoric that the region was becoming the very garden spot of American abundance. Grady in 1890 wrote rhapsodically: "Surely God has led the people of the South into this unexpected way of progress and prosperity. The industrial system of the South responds, grows, thrills with new life, and it is based on sure and certain foundations. For it is built at the field, by the mine, in the field—from which come the cheapest and best and fullest supply of cotton, iron and wood! . . . The industries of other sections—distant from the source of supply—may be based on artificial conditions that in time may be broken. But the industrial system of the South is built on a rock—and it cannot be shaken."

Events during the closing years of the nineteenth century and the opening years of the present century gave the illusion of fulfilling the New South dream. In the Piedmont South arose a textile industry that threatened to replace New England as the great center of American spindles and looms; in Birmingham arose an iron and steel industry that seemed to qualify it to be called the Pittsburgh of the South; in the cotton country arose a flourishing cotton oil industry; and in Texas and Louisiana arose one of the world's richest petroleum and chemical industries. At the same time, southern agriculture throve as new methods and fertilizers enabled small farmers to compete with planters in growing cotton, and as many landowners turned their capital and efforts to the production of cattle, fruit, or vegetables. In 1910 an English observer could have been speaking for the late Henry W. Grady in saying: "[This] great agricultural, industrial, and educational revival is rapidly transmuting the South from a ghost-haunted region of depression and impoverishment into one of the most eagerly progressive, and probably one of the wealthiest, of modern communities."

Meanwhile, the Progressive political movement that swept through the southern Democratic ranks in the early years of the twentieth century was an ideal vehicle for the cause of the New South. Southern progressivism reached high tide with the election of President Woodrow Wilson, a Virginia-born son of one of the founders of the southern Presbyterian church. The South voted solidly for Wilson, and he responded by establishing the most southern administration since the Civil War. Seven southerners held positions in Wilson's cabinets, and southern senators and congressmen played a dominant role in the enactment of the body of legislation that Wilson called the "New Freedom." Southern spokesmen played a strong part also in the events leading to the American entry into World War I and in supporting the military effort when war came. The fullness of southern participation in the conflict seemed to place a final seal on the covenant of national unity that had been temporarily broken by the secession of the South more than half a century before.

On the surface, the South of the post–World War I decade was in many ways indistinguishable from other parts of the country. Southern cities had their skyscrapers even if they were dwarfed by those of New York or Chicago. Southern metropolises had their continuous snarls of automobile and pedestrian traffic and noise. They hummed with commerce and a growing industry. The booster spirit was strong. If Grady had come to life in one of the larger southern communities, he would have believed his prophecies fulfilled beyond all his hopes.

But the national image of the South emphasized aspects of its behavior and appearance other than its integration into the American political, economic, and social mainstream. Nonsouthern views on the region were not altogether different from some of those cherished by southerners. Perhaps out of a sense of need to escape the stultifying effects of a rampant urban-industrialism, nonsoutherners helped keep alive the picture of the romantic Old South—the land of moonlight, magnolias, and mint juleps. There was also a less flattering image of the South that existed along with the romantic one in the nonsouthern mind. George B. Tindall has called this other image that of the "Benighted South."

The Benighted South was old stock in the great American morality theater. It began before the Civil War with the abolitionist crusade against slavery. Certainly this zealous reform movement was right in condemning forced servitude. But ultimately the accusations went far beyond this to become a raging philippic against an entire people and their culture. No area of southern life escaped the sting of northern politicians, editors, preachers. Southern politics, according to them, was an exercise in oligarchy and conspiracy, southern religion a blasphemy, southern education a mockery, southern family life a debauchery, southern character a morass of barbarism and degradation. In an abolitionist book on the southern Methodist church titled, significantly, *The Brotherhood of Thieves*, this denomination was said to be "more corrupt than any house of ill fame in New York." The whole South was referred to as "one great brothel." In blessing John Brown's attempt to incite the slaves to a general insurrection, Theodore Parker cried: "Virginia is a pirate ship, and John Brown sails the sea a Lord High Admiral of the Almighty with His commission to sink every pirate he meets on God's ocean of the nineteenth century." Professor Frank L. Owsley, a member of the Agrarian writers, once wrote: "One has to seek in the unrestrained and furious invective of the totalitarians to find a near parallel to the language that the Abolitionists and their political fellow travelers used in denouncing the South and its way of life. Indeed, as far as I have been able to ascertain," he continued, "neither Dr. Goebbels nor . . . other Axis propaganda agents ever so plumbed the depths of vulgarity and obscenity."

After the abolition of slavery and the defeat of secession in the Civil War, followed by a turbulent and recriminatory, but brief, period of Reconstruction, the North and South turned to the task of learning to live together in a reasonable state of amity. For a half century the southern image improved in the American mind because national unity, sectional reconciliation, was the imperative of the era. The romantic picture of the Old South and the optimistic picture of the New South became predominant in the North as well as in the South. Northern readers could not get enough of the writings of the southern local colorists. Three of the most thoughtful northern writers—Herman Melville, Henry James, and Henry Adams—wrote works in which southerners in the decades after the Civil War remained virtuous amid the crassness and venality of American life, especially that in the nation's capital.

Twentieth-century America inherited strong traces of

both images of the South, but by now the need for sectional comity no longer seemed so pressing. There were other imperatives, and the South was the most obvious deviant from the nation's image of itself. The South was the locale of the most visible practices of racial discrimination, religious fundamentalism, arrested cultural development, conservative politics, and retarded economy. The region was an irresistible target for the new century's outspoken social critics. It was the very favorite target of the most flamboyant of these critics, the popular Baltimore essayist, cynic, and lampoonist H. L. Mencken.

In 1917 Mencken opened fire with an essay in which he gave the South the name "Sahara of the Bozart." "One thinks of the interstellar spaces," he said, "of the colossal reaches of the now mythical ether. . . . It would be impossible in all history to match so complete a drying-up of a civilization." Later he wrote a piece calling the South the "Bible Belt," a scathing attack upon what he considered the narrowness and bigotry of its religious outlook, which he denounced as "Baptist and Methodist barbarism." "No bolder attempt to set up a theocracy was ever made in the world," he wrote, "and none ever had behind it a more implacable fanaticism." To him, Prohibition was the worst crime committed by the southern religionists. He said the passage of the Prohibition amendment to the federal Constitution caused southerners to gloat "in their remote Methodist tabernacles as they gloat over a hanging."

The occurrence in 1925 at Dayton, Tennessee, of the trial of a public school teacher for violating the state's antievolution law brought Mencken to the height of his denunciation of the South. Among other equally elegant expressions, he damned the area as the "bunghole of the United States, a cesspool of Baptists, a miasma of Methodism, snake-charmers, phoney real-estate operators, and syphilitic evangelists." Oddly, Mencken's outpourings seem to have eluded Professor Owsley's search for a parallel to the vulgarity and obscenity of the abolitionists.

All this, then, was the immediate setting for the emergence of the Agrarian authors. They lived in a South that was significantly behind the rest of the nation according to every measure of progress: a South that yet preserved a great body of its traditional beliefs and values: a South that bore a heavy burden of national scorn.

The Agrarians were, of course, scholars and men of letters in addition to being southerners. They were part of a world community of literary figures, such as Joyce and Eliot, many of whose ideas they shared. Professor Louis D. Rubin has wisely written that one should not read the Agrarians' manifesto, *I'll Take My Stand*, as a treatise on economics and politics or as a guide to regional social structuring. Instead, he says, one should read it as a commentary on the nature of man.

Yet the Agrarians *were* southerners, and their response to the world situation was unmistakably a southern response as well as a philosophical one. The issuance of their famous book was in part precipitated by the diatribes being hurled against the region. John A. Rice (a southerner, but not one of the Agrarians) once wrote that regardless of the many differences among southerners, there was a certain inner unity that became evident in the way they reacted to outside criticism. All southerners, he said, tended to boil at the same point. Various of the Agrarians have made clear that the Dayton trial and the ridicule of southern institutions caused by it brought them to the boiling point. In forming their reply, the Agrarians drew upon time-honored southern perceptions and convictions. Finally, they were responding to a mood of the South itself, because they saw that the modern advocates of a New South were about to abandon the "vital nexus" with the traditional South; that they were poised for a mighty effort to make the dream of industrial and material progress come true at whatever cost to other values. The Agrarians took this occasion to warn of the consequences before it was too late. Or so they hoped.

John Shelton Reed

For Dixieland: The Sectionalism of *I'll Take My Stand*

A sociologist—particularly a *Chapel Hill* sociologist—must feel some diffidence when contributing to what is quite naturally something of a celebration of the Vanderbilt Agrarians. As the historian I. A. Newby has written, "Next to Communists and industrialists, the Agrarians considered their chief antagonists to be [the] group of sociologists and regional planners at the University of North Carolina. . . ." There is no profit in raking up that old controversy: the Carolinians' prescriptions seem to have carried the day, but it is *I'll Take My Stand*, not Howard Odum's *Southern Regions*, that is still being read after fifty years. You have conquered, O Tennesseans.

Yet such competence as I have is as a sociologist, and I certainly have no desire, in this company, to treat the Agrarians as literary men. What I propose is to examine them sociologically, as a social movement of a particular sort: not in order to pigeonhole them, not to "explain" and thereby to diminish their achievement, but rather to draw attention to those things that they shared with other, similar movements. Since sociology has its limitations, as Donald Davidson was fond of pointing out, this approach can only make, at best, a limited contribution to understanding a complex movement, comprising a dozen exceedingly complex men.[1] But what a sociologist can do is to observe that, increasingly for the past two hundred years and now almost universally, circumstances like those Professor Roland describes in his essay lead some individuals very much like the Twelve Southerners to say things very much like what, on the surface, they appeared to be saying. If the Nashville group said these things better, or said something else besides, a glance at these other, similar movements may help us identify what was, in fact, unique about their statement.

One way to look at the Agrarians, and certainly a useful way, places them in a tradition of anti-industrial thought that goes back at least to Ruskin and Carlyle and the Maypole-on-the-village-green socialism of William Morris, extends through T. S. Eliot and the English Distributists, and can be found today in the work of such strange bedfellows as Paul Goodman, Ivan Illich, and E. F. Schumacher, with echoes from the governor of California and the *Mother Earth News*. Among the Agrarians' contemporaries, we can identify even such dyed-in-the-wool Yankees as Albert Jay Nock, whose sketch of the imaginary country of "Amenia" resembles the Agrarians' ideal more than incidentally, and Ralph Adams Cram, who had more success reviving Gothic architecture than Gothic thought, but very much admired the neo-feudalism of Franklin Delano Roosevelt and Benito Mussolini. (Cram's grandfather, to judge from his grandson's portrait, would have hit it off famously with John Don-

1 I recognize the difficulty of generalizing about this group of twelve individualists, and what I have to say will undoubtedly be more true of some than of others. The themes I will emphasize can be found in many of the essays in *I'll Take My Stand* and in its introductory statement, but they were developed more fully in the later writings of some of the contributors, notably Donald Davidson and Frank Owsley. Both implied at times that they were speaking for the group, and I shall take them at their word, since only H. C. Nixon saw fit to dissociate himself publicly from what they were saying during the thirties.

ald Wade's Cousin Lucius, for all that the old man was a New Englander.)

But as a specimen of this Anglo-American tradition, the Agrarians' writings were unusual in one very important respect: they did not have to look back to the Middle Ages or ahead to some envisioned sometime to see the realization of their ideal. No, they claimed that ideal was realized, or anyway had been realized until recently, or perhaps was almost realized—that it was incarnate right where they took their stand, in the American South. Their manifesto defended not only a way of life and an economic system they thought was necessary for it, but a particular region they believed embodied it. The South and agriculture seemed at the time to be joined intimately, if not inextricably, and there is no need to say which of the twelve loved the South because it was agrarian and which valued agrarianism because it was the South's way. I doubt that most could have said themselves, in 1930, and in any case no one had to say, until much later.

But to emphasize an obvious fact that we should not overlook, *I'll Take My Stand*—whatever else it may be—is a very *southern* book. Despite some well-known objections, the book was not called *Tracts Against Communism*, but took its title from the Confederate anthem. The authors were "Twelve Southerners," not Twelve Agrarians, Twelve Anti-Communists, or Twelve Poets. The book begins with the words: "The authors contributing to this book are Southerners. . . ." If we can believe some of the contributors, even its intended audience was exclusively southern.

It is easy to overemphasize this aspect of the manifesto, as did the critic who concluded that the Agrarians' economic ideas were "just a literary device, a periphrastic manner of expressing an emotion," and that, really, agrarianism was "simply the name for a discontent with the contemporary situation in the South." But it is equally wrongheaded to ignore the fact that most of the twelve were discontented with that situation, and did mean to grind some axes and air some grievances.

Among us Chapel Hill sociologists, that attitude is known as "sectionalism," and it made my predecessors—the Agrarians' adversaries—very uncomfortable. But a sociological analysis of *I'll Take My Stand* requires that we look at this aspect of it, and not just with alarm. A theory of sectionalism would help, but there is no such creature. There is another word, though, and a body of theory to go with it, for movements that seek to attain and to defend the integrity and the interests of ethnic or regional groups. Elsewhere in the world, we call that *nationalism*.[2]

That is the off-the-rack sociological category I want to measure the Agrarians for in this essay. Twenty years after *I'll Take My Stand*, Frank Owsley made my point better than I possibly could. "There is no question," he said, "that much of the bitter resentment of backward peoples in the Orient against, what they term . . . 'Yankee imperialism' is similar to that felt by the contributors to *I'll Take My Stand* in 1930." To understand the book, he insisted, it is necessary to recognize that it was not just a protest against industrialism, but equally a protest against the North's "brazen and contemptuous treatment" of the South "as a colony and as a conquered province."

2 Nationalism is often understood to imply a program of political independence for the alleged nation, but that is not a necessary or defining characteristic. Consider, for example, Flemish nationalism, which seeks protection and autonomy within Belgium, not independence from it. Cultural nationalism may develop into a movement for political independence, but even if that is the usual process, it is not an inevitable one. In any case, as I shall show, the "sectionalism" of the Agrarians did not rule out the demand for some indeterminate measure of political autonomy for the South.

If we ask what else the Agrarians had in common with those backward but anticolonial peoples in the Orient, and with other nationalists from Quebec to Kurdistan, if we examine *I'll Take My Stand* in the light of nationalist manifestoes from around the world, the similarities are obvious.

Consider first this business of grievances. Professor Sheldon Hackney has written that there is a sense of grievance at the heart of southern identity, and if he is right, there is no question that *I'll Take My Stand* is a very southern book in this respect as well.

The most obvious grievance was a cultural one. The Agrarians were not altogether persuasive, clear, or even agreed about what the South's culture was (who ever has been, for that matter?), but they did believe it was both threatened and looked down on by the rest of the United States, and by the industrial Northeast in particular. Whether or not the genesis of the movement is actually to be found in the Dayton "Monkey Trial," as some of the contributors have said, certainly the South had a bad press throughout the twenties, and these men were well aware of it. In a later essay, for example, Donald Davidson sketched what he took to be the characteristic view of the South from New York: "a region full of little else but lynchings, shootings, chain gangs, poor whites, Ku Kluxers, hookworm, pellagra, and a few decayed patricians whose chief intent is to deprive the uncontaminated, spiritual-singing Negro of his life and liberty." In *I'll Take My Stand* itself, Frank Owsley protested the smug prejudice of the North, which "still sits in Pharisaical judgment upon the South, beating its chest and thanking-Thee-O-Lord-that-I-am-not-as-other-men." John Crowe Ransom, for his part, lamented that the unreconstructed southerner was regarded as "quaint" and "eccentric"—"a rare exhibit in the antique kind [whose] position is secure from the interference of the police . . . but is of a rather ambiguous dignity."

The Agrarians were especially alarmed that southerners were in danger of absorbing northern views of their own history and culture. Allen Tate complained that things had reached the point where "Southern school children sing 'Land of the Pilgrims' Pride'"; Davidson criticized northern textbooks and models for "uprooting" southern students; and Owsley's description of the "war of intellectual and spiritual conquest" against the South deserves to be quoted at length:

> The rising generations read Northern literature, shot through with the New England tradition. Northern textbooks were used in Southern schools . . . —books that were built around the Northern legend and either completely ignored the South or insisted upon the un-righteousness of most of its history and its philosophy of life. One would judge . . . that the Puritans and Pil-grim fathers were the ancestors of every self-respecting American. Southern children spoke of "our Puritan fathers." . . . As time rolled on, the chorus of "John Brown's Body" swelled ever louder and louder until the lusty voices of grandchildren and great-grandchildren of rebels joined in the singing.

I'll Take My Stand was clearly meant to be the opening salvo of a counterattack in this spiritual and intellectual war. For Owsley, the professional historian, the task seemed straightforward, if not easy. The "crusade being levelled against the South," he said later, was "based on poor infor-mation, or bad reporting." So "to aid the South in its re-orientation and in a return to its true philosophy"—the purpose, he said, of *I'll Take My Stand*—it was simply a mat-ter of setting the record straight.

For some of the other contributors, the relation of the counter-myth they were constructing to the South's actual history was a bit more . . . subtle. Ransom's thoughts on the utility of myth had been a matter of record since his unorthodox defense of fundamentalist religion in *God Without Thunder*, and in *I'll Take My Stand* he not only acknowledged that "there are a good many faults to be found with the old South," but allowed that "it does not greatly matter to what extent the identical features of the old Southern establishment are restored," so long as there was an "establishment" of *some* sort, "for the sake of stability." Stark Young went even further: "Dead days are gone," he wrote, "and if by some chance they should return, we should find them intolerable." The task, in his view, was to develop "some conception of the end of living, the civilization, that will belong to the South." As for academic history—well, Young felt there was something to be said for believing even "lies," if their effect on conduct was uplifting.

All in all, for men widely believed to be defending the southern tradition, some of the twelve took a curiously insouciant attitude toward what it might actually be. Some of the others explicitly regretted parts of it: Tate, for instance, was clearly distressed that the South's religious tradition was what it was (hardly a traditionalist view in the ordinary sense of that word), while Henry Blue Kline apparently rejected even the *agrarian* component of the southern tradition, saying he would "resist any tendency to go too far 'back to the soil.'"

But whatever the content of the counter-myth was to be, whatever its relation to the actual facts of southern history and culture, the essayists of *I'll Take My Stand* were clearly concerned to forge a view of the South's past and its future that southerners did not have to be ashamed of, one that might even win some respect outside the region. Most were trying to be faithful to the facts, and the facts were that the great *differentiae* of the South were three—three R's, as it happens: race, religion, and rural life. On all three scores, the Agrarians recognized that the South was seen as backward and "un-American."

Oddly, perhaps, given the time and place, they largely ignored race. When it was mentioned, it was often (as in Robert Penn Warren's essay) in rather untraditional terms. I suppose that all of them were, at the time, segregationists: that is not the point. They did *not* base their defense of the South on its undeniable standing as the last great Western Hemisphere redoubt of white supremacy. (Other spokesmen for the South have not shared their scruples, or their tact.) Their defense of the South emphasized the last two of those three R's—religion and, especially, rural life. And they effected a sort of rhetorical alchemy, transmuting vice into virtue, proclaiming that backward is beautiful. And they did it, some of us think, very persuasively.

I do not suggest that this choice of a myth—this choice, in a way, of a tradition—was arbitrary, cynical, or merely rhetorical. For most of the twelve, I am sure, the revulsion at industrialism and secularism and all of the related "isms" was genuine and visceral. But this defense of a way of life for which they adopted the shorthand label "agrarian" did have some rhetorically useful consequences. In particular, it supplied a satisfying answer to the questions of dignity and self-respect with which the Agrarians, as southerners, were concerned. It even suggested that the South might be a beacon, an example for the rest of the world to emulate.

But the Agrarians wanted not only to identify and to refurbish the southern tradition, or anyway *a* southern tradition. They wanted to defend it—and if it was indeed linked to agriculture and to rural life, it was greatly in need of defense. The spread of industrialism menaced those aspects of southern life and, some of the twelve came to believe, its dominance debased them.

So here was an economic grievance, to add to the cultural one. The Agrarians argued only that farming *could* be an ennobling way of life; they were not naïve or stupid, and they recognized that it takes a great deal to ennoble some-one who is underfed and shackled with debt. As Ransom put it: "Unregenerate Southerners were trying to live the good life on a shabby equipment, and they were grotesque in their effort to make an art out of living when they were not decently making the living."

In *I'll Take My Stand*, most were unclear about why this situation existed, although they seemed to agree that Appomattox had something to do with it. (Ransom came perilously close to attributing it to defect of character.) After the book appeared, perhaps in response to those who sneered at their ignorance of economics, several of the twelve undertook to learn something of the subject, and their diagnosis later became much more sophisticated: they began to write knowledgeably about tariffs, about patterns of owner-ship and tenure, about property taxes, freight rate differen-tials, and international markets. Their generalized suspicion that somehow the North was to blame for the South's problems was elaborated into a full-fledged analysis of the South's "colonial economy."[3]

They began also to suggest programs. Lyle Lanier pro-posed to nationalize large, multiregional industries; Tate suggested worker control on what would now be called the "Yugoslavian" model; Davidson discussed what could be

---

3 I am almost certain that this analysis was taken over entire from a book pub-lished shortly after *I'll Take My Stand* by Rupert Vance, one of those Chapel Hill sociologists. Vance seldom used the phrase "colonial economy" again and largely avoided the subject altogether. When I asked him why, he told me that his analy-sis gave aid and comfort to "sectionalists." But he never said his analysis was *wrong*.

done with reform of corporate profits taxes; and Owsley, in an essay he said had been approved by "quite a number" of the twelve, outlined a plan of agrarian reform and redistribution which earned from one critic the label "kremlinesque" (although Owsley didn't go as far as W. T. Couch of Chapel Hill, who thought collective farms might be a good idea for the South).

But, as some realized from the start, to implement these or any other reforms required power—a degree of self-determination the South had not had since 1865. The South existed within a federal system dominated (as the Agrarians saw it) by the industrial interests of the Northeast. Why should those interests voluntarily acquiesce in attempts to limit their power? In the "colonial economy" view of things, why should they do anything for the South? They had an interest in keeping it a hinterland too poor to industrialize on its own, a supplier of raw materials, a good place to put branch factories that needed only unskilled labor, and (behind tariff walls) a captive market.

So add to the economic and cultural grievances a political one. It was all very well for the introductory statement in *I'll Take My Stand* to say that "the South [proposes] to determine itself" in order to protect its "minority right to live its own kind of life." But the manifesto said almost nothing about the form that self-determination was to take, or how it was to be achieved. Kline suggested the economic boycott and some sort of unspecified "civic and political activity" to discourage "promoters and exploiters"; Tate unhappily allowed that the only solution was "political, active, and, in the nature of the case, violent and revolutionary"; and Ransom suggested that if the South and its allies could not achieve a position of dominance within the union, then a "nasty" agitprop campaign, portraying industrialism as "a foreign invasion of Southern soil," might secure for the

South "a position in the Union analogous more or less to the position of Scotland under the British crown—a section with a very local and peculiar culture that would, nevertheless, be secure and respected."

But like the Scottish nationalists, some of the Agrarians came to believe that toleration was not sufficient. Both Davidson (in *Who Owns America?*) and Owsley (in that essay approved by "quite a number" of the others) called for what the British now call "devolution"—"a new constitutional deal," in Owsley's words, that would put most of the domestic functions of government in the hands of the regions.

From time to time, spokesmen for the Agrarians denied that they were rethinking secession, but some denied it rather unconvincingly. Both Owsley and Davidson, for instance, warned that something like their plan for regional autonomy was required if the United States was to endure. Davidson imagined some future historian lecturing on the 1930s, pausing to say "with emphasis" (and Davidson put these lines in italics): *"At this point regional differences passed beyond the possibility of adjustment under the Federal system, and here, therefore, began the dismemberment of the United States, long since foreshadowed in the struggles of the eighteen-sixties."* I cannot say how genuine was his distress at that prospect.[4]

In any case, we find in *I'll Take My Stand* all of the characteristic grievances—cultural, economic, and political—of a typical nationalist movement. And, especially if we follow the Agrarians past *I'll Take My Stand*, we find more than glimmerings of the typical nationalist responses: cultural defense, economic autarchy, even political self-determination.

4 In much of this, there was an element of posturing, even of playfulness, that makes it difficult to say how serious the Agrarians were, but some were obviously more serious than others. As Ransom wrote to Tate in 1932: "You know, our rebel doctrines are good for all of us but Don, and very doubtful there, because they are flames to his tinder." The same spirit can be observed, and the same difficulty arises, in the early stages of similar movements—Scottish, Québécois, or Occitanian nationalism, for instance.

So what? What profit is there in putting Ransom, David-son, and the others in a category that includes Herder, Maz-zini, and Ataturk; Kenyatta and Lévesque; Ho Chi Minh and Gandhi? (Never mind that Gandhi shared Andrew Lytle's enthusiasm for spinning wheels.) Even without the Agrar-ians in it, what use is a category as diverse as that?

To be sure, nationalism does come in a great many fla-vors: if not as many as there are nations, still enough to be confusing. But Anthony Smith, a British student of na-tionalist ideology, argues that we can identify a "core doc-trine" of nationalism, common to all, and distinct from the "supporting theories" that grow up around it.[5] Among the "themes that recur endlessly in the literature of national-ism" he finds "identity, purity, regeneration, the 'enemy,' historical roots, self-emancipation, building the 'new man' and the 'new community,' collective sovereignty and par-ticipation." These themes provide the motive for "the pecu-liar activities of nationalist movements"—the "philological, anthropological and historical researches of small coteries of intellectuals," for instance, or the "secret societies press-ing for reform and independence." (Devotees of Agrarian-ism will know of the Vanderbilt secret society with the rather ominous name of "Phalanx," which chartered a branch at the Normal School in Murfreesboro, and then lapsed back into a secrecy so profound that it has not been heard of since.)

Smith writes also of the virtually universal Golden Age, discovered in the nation's communal past, "a pristine state of true collective individuality," against which the present is measured and inevitably found wanting. But this Golden Age is not a strictly empirical description of past time; it is

5 These "supporting theories" may be romantic, liberal, theocratic, populist, nowadays even Marxist, and the nature of a nationalism's supporting theory is obviously not inconsequential. I hope, some other time, to develop the obser-vation that the Agrarians' "supporting theory" was unusual—an indigenous growth, as their frequent references to Calhoun suggest.

constructed to satisfy "present yearnings for an ideal community." Nationalism's envisioned future community "will not replicate that of the Golden Age, but it will recapture its spirit and set man free to be himself."

All nationalists search for "dignity" and for "roots," threatened or denied not by property relations and class antagonisms, but by elements alien to the subjected nation. And, as Smith puts it: "The recovery of self-respect must be preceded by a return to 'nature'—'as in the days of old,' when the community mirrored the conditions of nature and produced 'natural men.'" But nationalism is not an uncritical traditionalism. On the contrary, it is "an attack on tradition and modernity alike, insofar as they obscure and distort the genuine relationship of man with nature and with his fellow-man." It is "a vision of the future which restores to man his 'essence,' his basic pattern of living and being, which was once his undisputed birthright."

I have quoted Professor Smith at length because it seems to me that, as a description of what the Agrarians were up to, it would be hard to improve on this summary, written by a present-day British sociologist who has probably never heard of them. The point is that what has proved to be the lasting contribution of *I'll Take My Stand*, its vision of the good life, may be an immediate outgrowth of its authors' "sectionalism." The latter is not simply an accidental, and perhaps unfortunate, side issue. The Agrarians' myth of the South differs from other nationalist visions, not in its general outlines or in the impulse that produced it, but in the raw materials its creators had to work with, and the talent they brought to its making.

We can explore this analogy—parallel, model, call it what you will—a bit further.[6] Students of nationalism have of-

6 A pleasant parlor game can be played by extracting passages from Nehru, Sun Yat Sen, Mazzini, or Herder, and matching them with equivalent passages

fered a number of generalizations about their subject, and we can ask how well these apply to *I'll Take My Stand* and its authors. One of these generalizations is that many of the characteristics of nationalist thought can be traced to the characteristics of nationalist thinkers. The early stages of nationalist movements, for instance, are almost always dominated by young, urban, literary intellectuals. By those attributes and usually by others as well, these leaders are both alienated from the culture they seek to defend and marginal, if that, to the existing structure of political power. The common emphases of nationalist thought stem from those dilemmas, and (students of such movements argue) are attempts to resolve them.[7]

Consider, for instance, the link between nationalism and youth, a linkage evident even in the names of many movements: Young Italy, Young Ireland, Young Egypt, Young China, the Young Czechs, and the Young Turks. Although nationalists may grow old, few old people become nationalists. The task, after all, is to rejuvenate a culture (and the young are also unlikely to have much stake in the existing settlement). The Twelve Southerners were no different: indeed, one reviewer of *I'll Take My Stand* mocked them as "the young Confederates." One often forgets (at least I often forget) just how young they were. At the time of the Monkey Trial, their average age was thirty. Ransom, sometimes regarded as the movement's elder statesman, was thirty-five. When the book appeared, several of the contributors were still in their twenties. And consider "Phalanx":

from *I'll Take My Stand* and *Who Owns America?*. An earlier draft of this essay went on and on in that fashion, but I have deleted most of that material in this version.

7 Perhaps I should point out that, like any reductionist explanation of an ideology, this one does not address itself to the truth or justice of a nationalist viewpoint: rather, it seeks to explain why that position is held by one group rather than another, and in a particular situation.

student societies are an almost universal accompaniment to nationalism.

The theme of generational conflict is present in most nationalisms, at least in their early stages (until, we may suppose, some of the nationalists have time to age). The introductory statement to *I'll Take My Stand* calls on "the younger Southerners" to "come back to the support of the Southern tradition," and when Ransom appealed to "my own generation" to defend the South, he was still under forty. Nationalism's appeal to youth is often coupled with a rejection of old and traditional leadership, except for those leaders conveniently dead. I do not believe that *I'll Take My Stand* presents *any* living southerner as admirable, except for "William Remington," Henry Blue Kline's alter ego. Even the estimable Cousin Lucius—as Wade's sketch says, "Mas' Lucius done dead!" No, nationalists everywhere scorn those who, like most of us over thirty, have made their peace with oppression—which may put a new light on Ransom's contemptuous dismissal of "inept Southern politicians." And the well-known crack about the Fugitives' being in flight from "the high-caste Brahmins of the Old South" can be matched with the remarks of Indian nationalists who were "fleeing" *real* Brahmins.

The same scorn is directed at those fellow-nationals of any generation who fail to see the self-evident rightness of the nationalist analysis (and there are always many who do not see it, especially at first). One of the great appeals of nationalism is that, like all powerful modern ideologies, it can explain everything, including its own setbacks. So if southern newspapers, almost without exception, greeted *I'll Take My Stand* with ridicule or alarm—well, it was about what Owsley expected from organs "largely subsidized by Northern-owned power companies and Wall-Street-owned banks." And those southern intellectuals who were hostile to the Agrarians were, after all, "fawning for the favor of these [same] corporations or of other powerful Northern groups." Lytle also denounced the "modern scalawags who . . . openly acknowledge their servile dependence on New York" and "consciously or unconsciously" serve the interests of northern industry "for a small share of the booty." Almost identical passages could be multiplied endlessly from the literature of other nationalist groups.

Explaining rejection by the "folk" themselves is trickier. (Marxists, of course, have a similar problem.) Nationalists often argue that their nation has been degraded by its situation to the point where it cannot respond. We find similar themes in *I'll Take My Stand*. Young, for instance, argued that southerners have been disoriented by modernity, "by the World War and its aftermath; the churches, trying to keep up with the times . . . ; the schools; the moving-pictures; and, most of all, the press." He wrote of his friend, a doctor, who was "confused, like a child watching the train passing." Sometimes this line almost expresses contempt for the people one is trying to speak for. Nationalists have such high expectations for their people that they are often disappointed, and some wind up like Clemenceau, who is said to have loved France, but rather disliked Frenchmen. Among the Agrarians, Kline was probably least sympathetic with the "apathetic mass," "bovine-passive," but Ransom also had some hard things to say about "broken-down Southerners." It may be just as well for the Agrarians that so few ordinary southerners read their defense of the southern tradition.

The Agrarians themselves were not "ordinary" young southerners, and they knew it. Nationalists have nowhere been ordinary young people: the early stages of nationalist movements everywhere attract literary folk, which accounts for the emphasis Professor Smith observes on cultural is-sues—roots, and history, and national dignity, and self-re-spect. Nationalism is the original "single-issue politics," and its tendency to subordinate other issues accounts for the frequent difficulty of classifying it as "left" or "right," politically. The founders of nationalist movements, unlike the economists, engineers, and soldiers who often take over later on, are usually interested in political economy primarily as it impinges on cultural identity and what the Scottish Nationalists call "national self-respect." As an SNP tract puts it: "When the Scottish political renaissance has taken us to independence once again, then will be the time to take up left, right, or centre views."

When nationalists come from a nation that is economically "peripheral" in the world economy, one like the South of the 1920s that produced raw materials and supplied unskilled labor for a more "advanced" economy, they often adopt the same stance the Agrarians did, rejecting the Western sci-ence and technology that, in any case, they do not have, and insisting that their very backwardness in "Western" terms has preserved a spiritual and cultural superiority. From the nineteenth-century Slavophils, to the Hindu na-tionalists of early-twentieth-century India, to the apostles of *négritude* today, it is easy to find cases of Westernized intel-lectuals assuring the masses of peripheral nations of their superiority to those who dominate them economically and threaten to do so culturally.

Often we can observe the very same division that existed among the Agrarians between the "fundamentalists" (as Owsley called them) who wish to arrest industrialization al-together, and those others (among whom Owsley put him-self) who wish to domesticate industrialism and assimilate it to their valued culture. To be sure, we can find national-ists who positively lust to industrialize their nations, but

they often wish to do so in order to win international respect, and to bolster national self-respect. This motive was
not entirely alien to at least one of the Twelve Southerners: when Owsley proposed his program of reform, he remarked that "With such political economy, the South would
soon become one of the most important parts of the world."

And the Agrarians' emphasis on education and propaganda was absolutely typical of nationalist movements.
Their complaints about southern schoolchildren singing
"Land of the Pilgrims' Pride" read like nothing so much as
the complaints of Algerians forced to read about "our ancestors, the Gauls," or Indians raised on "our Anglo-Saxon
heritage." Nothing is more annoying than having someone
else tell you who you are. Control of education and the media—control of *mythology*—is probably the first nationalist
issue. Small wonder Marxists find them baffling.

Another characteristic of nationalists is that they are drawn
from precisely the least traditional elements of the nation.
Their educations, their occupations, their travels, and their
location in the cities distance them from the culture they
propose to defend. Moreover, they often *begin* at some distance from it: it is almost a commonplace that nationalists
are likely to be from the geographical fringes of their nation, and they are often from minority groups as well.[8]
Given the Agrarians' Vanderbilt setting, perhaps we should
not make too much of the fact that most of the twelve were
Kentuckians and Tennesseans, men of the upper and western South. But although Tate's mother allowed him to believe that he had been born in the Old Dominion until he
was thirty, the shameful fact is that there were no Virgin-

---

8 I collect examples, but will content myself here with two: the Ayatollah Kho-
meini, who grew up on Iran's border with India, and the One whom the Romans
crucified as "King of the Jews," who came from the first-century Palestinian equivalent of East Tennessee, as Nathanael reminds us in John 1:46.

ians or South Carolinians in the group, no one from what the residents of those states believe to be the spiritual heart of the Old South. In fact, there were very few—only three, I believe—from the Deep South, the old plantation belt that set the political tone of the South after Reconstruction.

It may be, in other words, that most of the Agrarians were *born* at some distance, geographically and psychologically, from the dominant tradition of the South. Certainly, as I have mentioned, their view of the South's tradition differed in its emphasis from the prevailing view a couple of hundred miles south of Nashville. As Professor Roland reminds us in his essay, it was U. B. Phillips, a Georgian, who insisted that "the central theme of Southern history and the cardinal test of a Southerner" was unwavering commitment to white supremacy.

It appears that someone has to stand at a certain remove from his culture in order to see it as something that can be dealt with, accepted or rejected by an act of the will, analyzed and *used*. And the Agrarians shared another experience that contributed to that distancing, one that has produced nationalists elsewhere: namely, the experience of having lived outside their native culture. "Exile is the nursery of nationalism," Lord Acton observed, "as oppression is the school of liberalism." And I believe that all of the twelve had lived outside the South before *I'll Take My Stand* was written.

The young provincial in the metropolis is a stock figure in many countries, and the experience does not even usually produce a nationalist. But when the provinces stand in a colonial or semi-colonial relation to the metropolis, when they have a distinct culture, when the provincial meets with rebuff or condescension, when he has the sensibility and the education to think about these matters ideologically—well, then the metropolis is asking for trouble. A student or professional may have removed himself from the provinces precisely in order to succeed, on the terms of the metropolitan culture. If he fails (or if he succeeds, but is not allowed to forget his origins). . . . The biographies of nationalists often reveal that they rejected the dominant culture only after it rejected them. Those who have seen the photographs of Gandhi decked out as an English solicitor will perhaps understand what I mean.

There are other ways being away from home breeds nationalism, besides reminding expatriates that they come from a culture viewed as inferior. In some part, we may see simply the politicization of homesickness. Michael Collins, an Irish nationalist, once tried to explain what he stood for: "Once, years ago, a crowd of us were going along the Shepherd's Bush Road [in London] when out of a lane came a chap with a donkey—just the sort of donkey and just the sort of cart that they have at home. He came out quite suddenly and quite abruptly and we all cheered him. No one who has not been an exile will understand me, but I stand for that." In *I'll Take My Stand*, Stark Young wrote, from New York, of the sort of experience that "brings tears to your eyes because of its memory of some place." "That place," he said, "is your country."

Being among people whose ways are different makes you aware of the ways you have left. Owsley learned a great deal at the University of Chicago that was not in the curriculum: some thirty years after *I'll Take My Stand* he still remembered what he had experienced as the absence of "the common courtesies of life." Kline also wrote of this experience: "William Remington" returned to the South to find "people living more nearly by his values and sensing life with sympathies closer to his own." And Ransom congratulated Tate in 1927 on his "stubbornness of temperament and habit," observing that he knew a great many like Tate, "born and bred in the South who go North and cannot bring themselves to surrender to an alien mode of life."

Finally, leaving home can make some things seem unimportant. Ernest Renan remarked in a famous essay on nationalism that the existence of a nation requires that a great many things be forgotten: in particular, those things that divide the nation. It is easier in London than on the Indian subcontinent to forget the history of mutual distrust between Hindu and Muslim, and African tribal differences may look insignificant from Paris, if not within the new African states themselves. Just so, from New York, Paris, or Oxford, yeoman and planter may have looked much alike, or at least their similarity may have seemed more important than the differences that were pretty much what southern politics was all about. (There is no evidence of it in *I'll Take My Stand*, but later some southern expatriates—Robert Penn Warren is one—have come to realize how much black and white southerners have in common.)

All of this is by way of saying that, for cultural nationalists, their tradition is not something that is second nature. Their experiences have left them like beached fish, aware for the first time of water. Their acceptance of tradition, their nationality itself, must be willed. In Tate's marvelously ambiguous phrase, they must take hold of their tradition "by violence."

Elie Kedourie is the student of nationalism who has put the matter in its starkest form. Modernization, he says, gives some young people the experiences and education to see their culture from "outside," as it were; it half-alienates them from that culture. At the same time, it provides them with the ideological vocabulary to interpret their alienation and to defend their culture, and modernization is itself what they protest. This alienation, this partial uprooting, is the motif that unites all of the generalizations about the characteristics of nationalist leaders. It is also conspicuously characteristic of most of the twelve Agrarians, as the North Carolina-born University of Chicago philosopher Richard Weaver pointed out in his essay "Agrarianism in Exile" some time ago. I will not belabor the point, but allow me simply to illustrate it, in the words of perhaps the least "modern" of the twelve, Donald Davidson.

In a lovely essay on sacred harp singing, Davidson came close to implying that the unexamined culture is the only one worth living in. Here is his description of the unself-conscious relation of the people of "Eden" to their culture: "The folks of Eden do not have to study much over what to keep and what to abandon, because they know how they wish to live. . . . Indeed, they do not particularly notice what they are keeping or make any great outcry pro and con." Compare that to Davidson's own attitude, expressed elsewhere: "We must recover the past, or at least in some way realize it in order that we may bring the most genuine and essential parts of our tradition forward in contact with the inevitable new tradition now in the process of formation." No Edenite could write that. Only someone who has been driven from the garden has the distance to treat its culture analytically, to speak of "parts of our tradition."

I have indicated how that distancing can come about, and a number of scholars have written about it, but few so well as Davidson—who could turn a nice bit of sociology himself, when he put his hand to it. He wrote once of the "moment of self-consciousness" that comes when a traditional society first faces modernization: "The invasion seems always to force certain individuals into an examination of their total inheritance that perhaps they would not otherwise have undertaken. . . . Their glance is always retrospective, but their point of view is thoroughly contemporary." The moment of self-consciousness is "the moment when a writer awakes to realize what he and his people truly are, in comparison with what they are being urged to become." Davidson was arguing that these conditions produce great literature, as in Ireland, Russia, and the South; but students of politics observe that they also produce nationalist movements.

And sometimes nationalist and artist are one and the same. When that is the case, what are intended to be tracts and manifestoes will speak to issues more important and more enduring than the ethnic or regional conflict that occasions them. *I'll Take My Stand* is such a volume. If it had been only a sectionalist broadside, it would not have the continuing, even increasing, importance it does appear to have.

Indeed, it would have very little importance of any sort, even historical, because as nationalist agitators the Agrarians were simply not very effective. As the thirties passed, they gained a few converts and rather more fellow-travelers, but many of the original twelve fell away—or perhaps "moved on" is the better phrase. In the essay I have mentioned, Richard Weaver, one of those fellow-travelers, had some perceptive things to say about why. As Weaver recognized, the parallels to other nationalist movements can be found there, as well. By the time of World War II, Agrarianism as a sectionalist movement was ailing, and it seems to me that the war and the fifteen years that followed, which emphasized American unity and American destiny—American nationalism—finished off the specifically southern aspects of the Agrarian protest. The same twenty years also completed the South's transformation into an urban and industrial society, and cut the ground from under anyone who sought to identify the southern way of life with agrarianism.

Let me close though, by observing one more common

feature of nationalist movements, a feature that may have some lessons for us. We can see, from outside or in retrospect, that the national tradition that nationalists take hold of is always selective, and sometimes selective to the point of distortion. The tendency is to oversimplify, to identify the nation with one aspect of its culture and to see everything else, wrongly, as dependent on that one aspect: the Russian church, the Chinese family, the German language—perhaps even the southern farmer.

But the reality is always more complex than an ideology can comprehend, and nations are more resilient things than most of their defenders acknowledge—as the Russian, Chinese, and German experiences in their different ways have shown us. George Orwell had some insightful things to say about nationalism, and about nations. He wrote once that it takes some very great disaster to destroy a national culture. In England, he said, "The Stock Exchange will be pulled down, the horse plough will give way to the tractor, the country houses will be turned into children's holiday camps, the Eton and Harrow match will be forgotten, but England will still be England, an everlasting animal stretching into the future and the past, and, like all living things, having the power to change out of recognition and yet remain the same."

I'll Take My Stand closed with some very similar thoughts about the South, the concluding lines of Stark Young's essay. In a volume celebrating the anniversary of that manifesto, I hope it is appropriate for one who shares the Agrarians' affection for the South to endorse those thoughts, and to close his essay with the hope that what Orwell said of England may be so for the South.

Lewis P. Simpson

The Southern Republic of Letters and
I'll Take My Stand

Cleanth Brooks, moderator of the Fugitives' reunion at Vanderbilt in May, 1956, opened the fourth session with an appeal for the assembled group to discuss "the poet in relation to culture, in relation to the South, in relation to the whole concept of community." A good deal of what was subsequently said bore on the rationale of the transition of four Fugitive poets—John Crowe Ransom, Allen Tate, Donald Davidson, and Robert Penn Warren—to the Agrarian movement. During the course of the debate, Tate offered the often cited opinion that Agrarianism "was religious humanism." Tate also made a more concrete observation, projecting an image of the Agrarian movement that seems to have passed unnoticed by the conferees and has remained so far as I know largely unremarked by the numerous students of Agrarianism. Tate said: "From the very beginning I thought of the Agrarian group as being rather like the French Encyclopedists. We issued certain ideas, reaffirmed the Southern tradition or standards. Well, the Encyclopedists turned out to be, according to the way you look at it, a great success. They brought on a revolution, or at least they provided the ideas for the revolution. And the Agrarian ideas didn't have such success. I think that's about all you can say about it." The comparison of the Agrarians to the

Encyclopedists was not merely fortuitous. Tate was recalling a vision of programmatic literary action that had glim-
mered before the eyes of Ransom, Tate, Warren, and himself in the months immediately before the active inception
of the Agrarian movement with the publication of *I'll Take
My Stand* in 1930.

In July, 1929, Davidson wrote to Tate (who was in France)
about "agitating the project of a collection of views on the
South, not a general symposium, but a group of openly partisan documents, centralizing closely around the ideas that
you, Ransom, & I all seem to have in common. It would
deal with phases of the situation such as the Southern tradition, politics, religion, art, etc., but always with a strong
bias toward the self-determinative principle. It would be
written by native Southerners of our mind—a small, coherent, highly selected group, and would be intended to
come upon the scene with as much vigor as is possible—would even, maybe, call for *action* as well as ideas."
Sparked by a fear, conveyed in the same letter from Davidson, that Howard Mumford Jones (then at the University of
North Carolina) was organizing a symposium of southerners devoted to progressivist principles, Tate thought "the
publication of a manifesto" desirable, but he envisioned
this as but preliminary to the execution of a revolutionary
"Southern movement"—elaborate, rigorously disciplined,
far reaching. He set forth his conception of this movement
in a letter to Davidson on August 10, 1929. (He had shortly
before conveyed the same message to Warren, a Rhodes
scholar at Oxford, whom Tate was obviously anxious to
bring into a more intimate connection with the burgeoning
revolutionary spirit of his three former colleagues in the
Fugitive group). Let me quote this communication at some
length. It is not easy to paraphrase and I do not want to lose
the tonal quality of what I think must be recognized not

only as a key document in the history of Agrarianism but in southern letters altogether; not only, moreover, in the history of southern letters but, more broadly, in the history of American letters, and still more inclusively, in the history of modern Western letters.

> I have recently had news [Tate writes] of your activities in behalf of a Southern movement. . . .
>
> The other day I wrote to Warren, and suggested the following tactical program:
>
> 1. The formation of a society, or an academy of Southern *positive* reactionaries made up at first of people of our own group.
>
> 2. The expansion in a year or two of this academy to this size; fifteen active members—poets, critics, historians, economists—and ten inactive members—lawyers, politicians, private citizens—who might be active enough without being committed at first to direct agitation.
>
> 3. The drawing up of a philosophical constitution, to be issued and signed by the academy, as the groundwork of the movement. It should be ambitious to the last degree; it should set forth, under our leading idea, a complete social, philosophical, literary, economic, and religious system. This will inevitably draw upon our heritage, but this heritage should be valued, not in what it actually performed, but in its possible perfection. Philosophically we must go the whole hog of reaction, and base our movement less upon the actual old South than upon its prototype—the historical social and religious scheme of Europe. We must be the last Europeans—there being no Europeans in Europe at present.
>
> 4. The academy will not be a secret order; all the cards will be on the table. We should be *secretive*, however, in our tactics, and plan the campaign for the max-

imum of effect. All our writings should be signed "John Doe, of the —— ——," or whatever we call it.

5. Organized publication should be looked to. A newspaper, perhaps, to argue our principles on the lower plane; then a weekly, to press philosophy upon the passing show; and, third, a quarterly devoted wholly to principles. This is a large scheme, but it must be held up constantly. We must do our best with what we can get.

The advantages of this program are the advantages of all extreme positions. It would immediately define the muddling and *unorganized* opposition (*intellectually* unorganized) of the Progressives; they have no *philosophical* program, only an emotional acquiescence to the drift of the age, and we should force them to rationalize into absurdity an intellectually untenable position. Secondly, it would crystallize into opposition or complete allegiance the vaguely prosouthern opinions of the time. These two advantages of my proposed academy seem to me decisive. Without the academy we shall perish in two ways: (1) under the superior weight of metal (not superior strategy) of the enemy (Progressives); and (2) our own doctrine will be diluted with too many shades of opinion.

In short, this program would *create an intellectual situation interior to the South*. I underscore it because, to me, it contains the heart of the matter.

For the great ends in view—the end may be only an assertion of principle, but that in itself is great—for this end we must have a certain discipline; we must crush minor differences of doctrine under a single idea. I suggest a repudiation of Jefferson and a revised restatement of the South Carolina idea. We shall never refute Progress with the doctrine of a man whose negative side made Progress possible. Jefferson's system (!) was made to oppose an illusory monarchy in the U.S.

> In short we cannot merely fight centralization; we must
> envisage a centralization of a different and better kind.
> In fact, we must here oppose one of the ideas of the
> Southern tradition. Emotionally this does me consider-
> able violence because I am, emotionally, a Jeffersonian.
> This is what I mean by discipline.
>
> Another and greater Southern movement foundered
> on indiscipline of ideas. I refer to the Montgomery
> Convention of February, 1861. Study it and take warn-
> ing. Those men *felt*, but they would not *think* through
> habits and political inertia. The Montgomery Conven-
> tion lost us the war. There was no one to tell them the
> logical consequences of their position. We must take
> logic to the most extreme ends, and then perform what
> we can. . . . *Organization and discipline are indispensable.*

A contradiction between means and ends in Tate's program for the South is clear: the employment of tactics usually associated with Enlightenment progressivism to promote reaction against progressivism. It may be less clear
that this contradiction is significantly implicated in the relation Tate's program for a southern movement bears to the
Enlightenment symbolism of literary and intellectual order.
I refer to a more or less hidden suggestion by Tate. This is to
the effect that the failure of an older southern movement,
the Confederacy, to achieve its revolutionary aims is at-
tributable to a subtle alienation of the men of letters who
instituted the Republic of the Confederate States of America; an alienation not only from the original American Republic but from an invisible republic on which the Republic
founded in 1790 was in a real sense modeled—that is, the
symbolic dominion of secular mind, the third realm in the
Western orders of civilizational existence, the Republic of
Letters. I am somewhat painfully aware, let me observe at
this point, that I have remarked on the Third Realm and

American (including southern) writers a good deal. My return to the subject is with the intention of suggesting more comprehensively—and I hope more forcefully—than I have before that a major historical context of the Agrarian movement is the southern implication in the Third Realm.

Indicating the heart of his program in the letter to Davidson—the notion of creating an organized and militant intellectual situation interior to the South—Tate, it is to be observed, does not indicate a state of mind committed to a restoration of the antebellum South. The intellectual situation he proposes to establish would substantially consist in the recognition of and the rectifying of the South's failure to conform to its social prototype, the old European community. Although this community was destroyed by the French Revolution and cannot be restored on its own ground, Tate seems to say, the descendants of the Europeans transported to another ground, the American South, still possess the capacity to be Europeans and so to restore the true European scheme. His subscription to this notion was recalled by Tate years later (at the 1956 reunion) when he compared the Agrarians to the Encyclopedists. The Encyclopedists were engaged in placing society under mind's control; the twentieth-century southern intellectuals of the Agrarian persuasion were engaged in enlisting mind against itself in a reversal of the revolution enacted by the philosophes. The southerners would, let us say, encourage mind to reverse its status, to become as it once had been: the consciousness of the webbed order of myth and tradition, always submissive to ritual, manners, and customs; a consciousness poetic, philosophical to an extent, but not capable of self-analysis—the consciousness of a society of men existing under the complete sovereignty of God (or gods).

Although he identified his intention with a southern

movement located specifically in the context of the failed War for Southern Independence and its aftermath, what Tate aimed at was not so much to create an intellectual situation peculiarly interior to the American South but to bring into full expression the southern representation of the intellectual situation interior to Western civilization. In other words, Tate intended to join a movement of men of letters in the American South to the central motive of modern Western letters: a paradoxical and aggressive movement of mind against itself. This motive, I shall presently observe, is to be divined as a shaping impulse of *I'll Take My Stand*, which in its inward meaning is an attempt to reverse the roles of mind and society as models of existence. It is a document, in other words, that would have done its work and then, along with the movement that made it, have, as they say on the Buck Rogers show or somewhere, "self-destructed."

But I am getting ahead of the story. Let me move back toward, if not the, at any rate a beginning.

The symbolism of literary order originated primarily in a tension between mind and society as symbols of order—a tension produced by the process, as Hegel describes it, of secularizing the spiritual, a phenomenon attendant upon the exodus of the medieval "clerks" (I am thinking of Julien Benda's noted use of the term in his *La trahison des clercs* in the 1920s) from the *res publica Christiana* to an emergent, secular *res publica litteraria*.

The prototypical literary movement, marking an unparalleled differentiation of the spiritual from the secular, this exodus is the beginning of modern history.

Singularly literary—uniquely shaped by and dependent on the secular use of letters—this period of history, *i.e.* modern history, may presently be undergoing a differentiation into another age of history. We do not know what this other time will be like. But we yet live with the chief assumption of modern history: namely, that the model of history is mind; that history is a grand, willful process—conducted by rational, secular mind—of transferring all that the human consciousness comprehends as existence into itself. We further assume that the agency of this continuing process is a great critique of man and society, nature and God, and finally of mind itself. We further assume that this agency is the animating spirit of the dominion resulting from the exodus of the clerks, the Republic of Letters—a universal polity of secular mind, a realm additional to the realms of Church and State and independent from them, in short a third realm in the Western orders of civilizational existence. The Great Critique is not simply the prototypical literary movement (there having been no literary movements in classical or medieval times, or before the differentiation of a realm in which they may occur); it is in an overall sense the only literary movement. It has tended, however, to become highly complex; indeed, embracing many "fields of science" on the one hand and numerous "fields of literature" on the other, it has become so fragmented that we have difficulty seeing that in its very fragmentation it retains an intrinsic unity. The movement into mind preserves its character as a movement out of the spiritual into the secular—a movement (as Hegel observes) in which the secular takes on the aspect of what it displaces. The vocation to secular letters bears the imprint of the vocation to the sacred: the secular, historical self of the modern writer is a painful differentiation from the self as an immortal soul and retains the imprint of the self as soul. The aura of the clerk and priest surrounds the wholly secular man of letters. In fact, the tension within the act of transferring man and God into mind generated such a powerful drama of self and history within the Great Critique that this became the subject of literature (of what Edgar Allan Poe called "literature proper"). From Shakespeare, Bacon, and Cervantes on, the Great Critique—whether expressed in poetry, fiction, drama, the essay, formal or informal—has found a basic unity in its recording of the drama of secular mind's embodiment in the self: in the self's experience of the movement of man and society, nature and God—and not less the soul—into mind, in the drama of the self's internalization of history. As symbolic prototypes of the poet and the man of letters, Hamlet, Prince of Denmark, and Don Quixote, the Knight of the Sad Countenance, record the drama of the soul's search for survival through a poeticizing of its devastating experience of transformation into the secular, historical self. The melancholy prince and the melancholy don become world historical figures—depictions of the first poets to know the modern intimacy between the self and history, of the first poets to know not only an isolation of the self in history but an isolation of history in the self.

The dramatic crux of Hamlet's and Don Quixote's internalization of history is its prophetic intimation of the failure of society as the model of history; and, what is more significant, the ominous suggestion that a self-willed resistance to history represents not only an enclosure of self in history and an enclosure of history in self but the possibility that the struggle of the lonely self to, like Hamlet, repair a "time . . . out of joint" has become the model of history.

At bottom both Shakespeare and Cervantes are motivated by a tension toward the dread knowledge that the displacement of society by mind is irreversible.

The eminent contemporary representative of mind, Sir Francis Bacon, confirmed this knowledge joyfully. It was the basis of his confident and decisive assertion: "Knowledge is power."

The full realization of the reversal of society and mind was not to occur, however, until the phenomenon was actually incarnated in an historical act; in the invention of the American Republic, which brought into existence a society, unique at that point in history, a society modeled on rational, secular mind. The American Revolution was the first decisive fulfillment of the literary movement that, issuing out of the subjectification of nature, society, and God, became the Great Critique. In terms of American history, the American Revolution and its manifesto, the Declaration of Independence, together with other crucial Revolutionary texts—the writings of John Adams, Thomas Paine, Philip Freneau, *et al.*—constitute both the first literary movement in America and a culmination of the Great Critique, or of the general literary movement that is modernity.

But in this act of mind there was a major historical irony. In its full-fledged, its first pragmatic, imposition of its will on history—not made for more than a century and a half after Shakespeare and Cervantes—mind sought to become the model of a slave society; of the society of the Atlantic seaboard colonies of the British empire—of all of them but most particularly of the southern tier of colonies, the "planting colonies." And of these most notably, Virginia, where chattel slavery made its initial appearance. Here slavery was an aspect of the secularity of a colony that early lost the religious impulse to colonization and turned more to the cultivation of tobacco than the propagation of faith—turned too, more than has been supposed (as Richard Beale Davis has shown in detail), to the cultivation of mind. The arrival of the first slave ship in Virginia anticipated the joining of mind and slavery in the creation of an intellectual situation interior to the historical evolvement of a series of colonial outposts into an independent nation. It is no historical accident that one of the greatest of the Enlightenment philosophes, Thomas Jefferson, was a Virginia slavemaster.

In its underlying meaning the Declaration of Independence is an interpretation of history as having culminated in the reversal of society and mind; it is a metaphorical announcement of mind's assumption of dominance over society by means of its embodiment in the sovereign self. But, having proclaimed its triumph over society in the Declaration, mind immediately united itself with society's ancient way of working its will. Sealing its interpretation of history in battle and blood, mind—as represented by Jefferson and others—intimated all too presciently that as it became the source and model of history its interpretations, often divided against themselves, would become bloodier and bloodier.

Experiencing its singularly intense embodiment of mind under the American conditions, the self experienced an intimacy with history it had not before known. This experience became even more intense as mind, committed to the unremitting criticism of all phases of human existence, extended its interests to itself and began a radical exploration of its own existence. In America one result of this exploration is to be seen in New England, where Transcendentalism provoked a flight of the self from history into the Oversoul. A different result is to be seen in the South, where a special version of the modern society—of the society of science and history—ironically identified intellect, letters, and slavery; and indeed made the preservation of slavery as an institution more dependent on this unique identification than on the identification of slavery with race. The recognition of the relation between literature and slavery was, in fact, as Alexis de Tocqueville points out in the first volume of *Democracy in America*, the chief feature of the South's "peculiar institution." Noting that Americans in the South have "bettered the physical conditions" of slavery, Tocqueville observes that in another way they have committed an atrocity without parallel: "The only means by which the ancients maintained slavery were fetters and death; the Americans of the South of the Union have discovered more intellectual securities for the duration of their power. They have employed their despotism and their violence against the human mind. In antiquity precautions were taken to prevent the slave from breaking his chains; at the present day measures are adopted to deprive him even of the desire for freedom. The ancients kept the bodies of their slaves in bondage, but placed no restraint upon the mind and no check upon education. . . . But the Americans of the South, who do not admit that the Negroes can ever be commingled with themselves, have forbidden them, under severe penalties, to be taught to read or write."

In an earlier age, before the invention of printing and the more general diffusion of literacy, the man of *no* letters had been associated with the culture of society; the man *of* letters had been associated with the clerks, and later as it developed, the rising realm of secular letters. In the contrast between them, the man of no letters and the man of letters defined each other. No such simple distinction could be made between the southern man of letters and the slave. The slave was not a man of no letters because of birth or lack of education; he was expressly forbidden the knowledge of letters, for however successful mind might be in shaping a slave society, it constantly feared—all "scientific" arguments relegating the Negro to an inherently inferior status notwithstanding—that the slave would acquire the power to shape society according to the will of intellect. The slave could not be allowed to learn to read and to write lest, embodying knowledge in the self, he enter the Republic of Letters and become an interpreter of history. Logically the best way to keep the slave far away from the precincts of the polity of letters was not by legislative prescription but by removing the institution of chattel slavery from any association with mind—with the society of history and science—and placing it within the context of an "organic society," in which all institutions are living parts of a ritualistic social order authorized by tradition and sanctioned by a coherent religious myth. So antebellum southern men of letters essayed at times to invent a South that represented a reversal of mind and society, none so energetically as the eccentric and prolific George Fitzhugh of Port Royal, Virginia. In his treatise entitled *Sociology for the South, or Failure of a Free Society* (1854) Fitzhugh drew the distinction between an "organic society" and the society of history and science.

> State governments, and senators, and representatives, and militia, and cities, and churches, and colleges, and universities, and landed property, are institutions. Things of flesh and blood, that know their rights, "and knowing dare maintain them." We should cherish them. They will give permanence to government, and security to State Rights. But the abstract doctrines of nullification and secession, the general principles laid down in the Declaration of Independence, the Bill of Rights, and Constitution of the United States, afford no protection of rights, no valid limitations of power, no security to State Rights. The power to construe them, is the power to nullify them.

Standing entirely against the principle of self-determination, Fitzhugh had the self-conscious intention of repudiating Locke and Jefferson and all interpreters of history, including (as Drew Gilpin Faust observes in an important recent study) the interpreters of the South's history who belonged to the William Gilmore Simms circle of antebellum literary intellectuals. But one of the subtly important facts of southern history is the fact that Fitzhugh was not truly opposed to the "men of mind" (to use Simms's term) of which Simms was more or less the center. The Simms group, according to Professor Faust's persuasive argument, shared with one of their number, George Frederick Holmes, a vision of making the South nothing less than the scene of an "intellectual reformation analogous to the Instauration Magna of Lord Bacon." Since the Renaissance, Holmes held, the intention of the *Novum Organum* had been corrupted: "The experimental philosophy has been the only part of his [Bacon's] labours that has been cordially accepted, and the Baconian instauration, thus shrunk and withered has been made at once the tool and the divinity of the age." Unjustly narrowed to an empiricist, Holmes stated, Bacon has been used to justify the "triune divinity of the nineteenth century, man, matter, and money." Eagerly embracing the need for "a new social science . . . designed to illuminate transcendent moral and social laws that simultaneously proscribe and foretell the future course of society," the Simms circle, Professor Faust points out, conceived the foundation of the southern instauration to be a new version of history. As Holmes put it, "A necessary preparation for a complete . . . Renovation of Knowledge would be a Philosophical History of the Intellectual, Moral, Social and Political Progress of mankind." Regarded as a "series of Experiments" that afford a basis for selecting the "principles . . . based on truth," such a history would provide a secure platform for society.

It was a bold vision the Simms circle had. It would make immanent in the American South "the transcendent moral and social laws that simultaneously proscribe and foretell the future course of society." Making the self-interpretation of a modern slave society the reinvigorating model of the society of history and science and the index to the future, it would make the South a symbol of mind. Paradoxically, however, it is to be doubted that in its essential motive the concept of the South as symbol of mind was counter to Fitzhugh's vision of the South as a revival of a patriarchical society. Fitzhugh's vision, to be sure, was basically the product of what it ostensibly denied, the power of intellect and letters. Indeed Fitzhugh, as he tacitly admitted, was as much the literary intellectual and self-conscious interpreter of history as abolitionists like William Lloyd Garrison and Horace Greeley. He was if anything more intensely the self-conscious man of letters than Simms. A reactionary sociologist and idealogue of patriarchicalism, aware that he must construe against all construing, Fitzhugh nullified all allegiance to the symbols of the interpretative mode of history, among them the Declaration of Independence and the Constitution of the United States, and too of course the inclusive symbols of the interpretative mode, the Great Critique and the Republic of Letters. But, ironically, in his rejection of the rational mode Fitzhugh was rigorously rational. Modeling the society of the South on the image of an organic order, he acted as the inheritor of the Great Critique. In common with Holmes, Simms, and others he exemplified an intellectual situation in which the free and autonomous mind had become the source and model of a slave society. The antebellum southern men of letters represented a more numerous and stronger literary talent than we have commonly granted. But compelled more and more to associate themselves with the preservation of slavery, they in effect progressively denied the literary and intellectual realm that was the homeland of the American Republic. In the American South the secularization of the spiritual realm, from which the modern man of letters had emerged some three or four hundred years earlier, was truncated: its evolvement into the phase when, as Hegel said, "secular pursuits become a spiritual vocation," and (in Carlyle's words) Literature assumes the status of the modern Church, was arrested. The literary mind in the South failed in the fundamental motive of the modern literary mind, to symbolize the Third Realm. Yet in this failure, it may be said, the writer in the South knew more keenly than his counterpart in New England the literary mind's identity with history. In New England the literary mind was not so nakedly exposed to history, for there it had a reference, if not to a traditionalist order, to what was an assumed order. In the nineteenth century Oliver Wendell Holmes could write a poem like "The Wonderful One Hoss Shay"; Longfellow could write "The Courtship of Miles Standish"; Hawthorne could write *The Scarlet Letter*. In the South Simms wrote strangely nostalgic romances about the American Revolution. More than the New England writer, the writer in the South experienced the association of the self with history. This is a preeminent significance of Edgar Allan Poe. Symbolizing the loss of society as the guiding authority for mind, his poems and stories record the drama of mind's transfer of itself into itself and what is consequent upon this, mind's accelerating consciousness of itself—its consciousness of consciousness, which includes a consciousness of the shadowy, vast domain of unconsciousness. In Poe's work the self learns that history is consciousness and consciousness is history. Still, for all his awareness of the terrors deriving from such knowledge, Poe does not suggest a rebellion of mind against its will to persist in the transference of mind into mind. His last work, "Eureka," is a vision of self-consciousness as the embodiment of the history of the universe.

The Civil War was the defeat of the first government ever created by the self-conscious literary mind and modeled on the self-conscious literary intelligence. A symbol of the triumph of mind, the American nation, with the firing on Fort Sumter, became a symbol of the defeat of mind. But at the end of the war the victorious North had achieved bloody ratification of its version of the society of history and science and could claim to be the vindication of rational order. The South was left to serve as the symbol of the defeat of mind in America. And, it must be said, the postbellum southern men of letters tended to oblige in such a service. Glorying in the defeat of mind, the literary redeemers let the capacity of criticism lapse. Putting literary endeavor to the service of a vision of the vanquished Confederacy and the perpetuation of a Lost Cause, postbellum southern writers with virtual explicitness refuted the South as a society of history and science modeled on mind. Uniting Church, State, and Letters in a vision of a South of mystical wholeness (a "City of the Soul," as Robert Penn Warren has termed it), they made the South a culture of memory. This culture held that what has been lost in history is merely apparent loss, that memory redeems the truth that historical interpretation has ruled obsolete or destroyed. The postbellum southern writers illustrate a phenomenon that may be observed more than once in modern times. A society that has failed in war and the shedding of blood to confirm its intellectual interpretation of itself as its own version of the society of history and science seeks its resurrection in a transcendent myth of its existence. A society of mind invents a myth of itself and completes the secularization of the spiritual by spiritualizing itself as a society of myth and tradition. The first manifestation of this phenomenon, I suppose, was the emergence of the France of Emperor Napoleon I out of the bloody civil and foreign strife, in which the revolution of reason and the rights of man generated by the Encyclopedists had failed of ratification. In the more extreme manifestations of this phenomenon—as in Mussolini's Italy or, far more terribly, in Hitler's Germany—a society of mind became a pseudo society of blood and cosmic mystery.

Although the full consequences of the South's resurrection as the Republic of the Lost Cause cannot even yet be assessed—may not yet have appeared—we see easily enough that in the period between the Civil War and the First World War many southern writers were hardly involved in an "intellectual situation." Insofar as they subscribed to the Republic of the Lost Cause, they belonged to a dominion that was beyond criticism and engendered no critical thought. Their mission was to endow secular society not only with the form but the essence of a spiritual kingdom, as witness Thomas Nelson Page's epitome of the Republic of the Lost Cause in an address in the 1880s:

> [The South] was crucified; bound hand and foot;
> wrapped in the cerements of the grave; laid away in the
> sepulchre of the departed; the mouth of the sepulchre
> was stopped, was sealed with the seal of government,
> and a watch was set. The South was dead, and buried,
> and yet she rose again. The voice of God called her
> forth; she came clad in her grave-clothes, but living,
> and with her face uplifted to the heavens from which
> had sounded the call of her resurrection.

But while the Lost Cause sponsored the illusion that the South had become a world in which mind and society had been reversed—a world in which mind was the servant of society—the activity of the critical mind did not altogether cease in the defeated South. It showed itself in Alexander H. Stephens and Jefferson Davis—in all the long tedious devotion to the justification of the Confederacy as a government modeled on mind. It demonstrated itself in an old fire-eater like Albert Taylor Bledsoe, who founded the *Southern Review* in Baltimore, a periodical that mingled argument about states' rights with the assertion of the philosophy of history as "the education of mankind." But most of all, in any writer we may associate with the postbellum South, criticism manifested itself in Mark Twain, who—owing to the circumstances of his birth and his career, both an insider and an outsider in his relation to the South—came to experience the ironies of the intellectual situation interior to the South, and to America, as no writer before him. His stories are close to being direct symbols of this situation. They move, the best of them—and surely in the greatest, *Adventures of Huckleberry Finn*—toward the revelation that society as created by mind is intrinsically a slave society. In the total sense, for it enslaves everybody. In Huckleberry's deeply personal account of his flight from what he cannot escape, his involvement in and unbreakable commitment to the American society invented by rational, secular mind, the only person who is capable of acting with any degree of moral freedom is Jim the slave. And this no more than momentarily. Ironically represented by a semiliterate child of the Missouri frontier, alienation from the society modeled on mind proves to be no escape from it. As represented by Huck, even a poetic estrangement—an inner exile—from society is frustrated by an immutable identity with history. When we consider that Huck, the teller of his own tale in his own language, is a parodic but wholly serious portrayal of the writer's sense of self and history, we realize how in

Huckleberry Finn Mark Twain has dramatized the abortive striving of literary mind to redeem itself from itself—to deny its identity with the society of mind. In the years following *Huckleberry Finn*, Mark Twain became progressively more desperate about the situation of the literary sensibility. Like Henry James and Henry Adams, he kept trying, as in *What Is Man?* and other fragmentary works of his later career, to define the inwardness of his condition as a writer. The search led him into the attempted composition of the novel usually referred to as *The Mysterious Stranger*. In this story his assignment of the role of the artist to Philip Traum, the nephew of Satan (or perhaps Satan himself), is a way of transcending history by art. Philip Traum in fact represents a satanic divinization of the creative power of art and an utter repudiation of both society and mind—of society as a reference of rational intellect and of intelligence as a model of society. Like the later work of Henry James, *The Mysterious Stranger* is a metaphor of the climactic movement of the self into the inwardness of history. The dreaming mind of the storyteller is united with the mind of the great artificer of consciousness, the supreme intellect and the supreme dreamer.

By the 1920s the efficacy of the writer's embodiment of mind had come thoroughly into doubt. To be sure, the literary impugnment of mind—of its motives, of its general reliability, of its validity as a model of society—approached completeness. In Yeats, Pound, Proust, Joyce, Eliot, the failure of the Great Critique became the major subject of the Great Critique; the failure of mind became the subject of mind. In the name of the power and nature of poetic knowledge, the literary mind became hypercritical of intellect as the source and model of history and society. But the role of mind was not effectively reduced. Far from subordinating itself, literary mind developed further its tendency to a self-conscious alienation from society; and justified this—Joyce is the great example here—as its effort to disclose itself to itself.

Mind, self, letters, and history: as the complex pressures and counter pressures of these elements of existence in high modernism urged the literary mind to halt the process of transference and somehow to reverse it, there developed an intellectual situation—embodied in the autonomous selves of a series of great literary artists and located at the deep core of modern literature—that engendered a maximum tension between the claims of mind and those of society. Succinctly revealed in Eliot's poems, at once personal and private and public, this was a situation in which the writer was a participant in a struggle to redeem the symbolic literary order, the Republic of Letters, as the model of history; and yet was acutely aware of an impulse to reject it, even to destroy it. The writer—as it were, the clerk—was aware of a desire to return to the service of a society of myth and tradition. But no writer could really imagine returning home from the exodus into the Third Realm. The literary mind, having made the Third Realm into a symbol of alienation from the society of history and science, opposed its interpretation of history to that of the scientific and technological mind, which by the second half of the nineteenth century had clearly set up in business for itself. No longer synonymous with the terms *letters* or *literature*, mind in the aspect of science had taken over the symbolic realm of mind; and, as Henry Adams and H. G. Wells say, having appropriated the Baconian slogan "Knowledge is power," had established itself as the interpretant of history, the goal of which had become the making of a world historical society fashioned entirely in the image of scientific mind. There was no longer any sense of alienation in "scientific mind"; it was at one with what it was making, the industrial-technological society. Meanwhile, the poets, like Eliot in "The Waste Land," envisioning the First World War as having ratified the world historical goal of the scientists in an unprecedented bloodletting, saw by the same token the grim confirmation of their historical alienation from the world.

What the poets—I mean those who seek to define existence through enactments of the imagination instead of through observation and experiment—most wanted to do in their twentieth-century situation was to establish the power of poetry as knowledge. In this they wanted nothing new. Wanting to do what poets had been trying to do ever since their exodus out of the medieval society into the Third Realm—to equate poetry and intellect and establish poetry as the criticism of society—they sought their image in the figure of the "poet-critic." From Ben Jonson on the poet-critic has self-consciously projected the symbolic reversal of mind and society in versions of pastoral, knowing that the pastoral reversal, although incredible as a pragmatic historical possibility, is of tactical value in the struggle to control the symbolism of the Third Realm and confer authority on the vocation to poetry. Twentieth-century poets envisioned mind reverting to bardic and/or meditative functions, and, paradoxically, through such passive modes of expression exerting an active authority on the direction of history (which is to say, of consciousness).

In his letters to Warren and Davidson—if I may return to the beginning of my discussion—Tate conceived a decided heightening of the pastoral tactic followed by the literary mind as it has pursued its strategic advocacy of society (as opposed to mind) as the proper model of history. In his programmatic statement of the methods necessary to a southern movement, Tate reflects the presumed, even the

overt, intention of *I'll Take My Stand*, anticipating the manifesto's formulaic declaration of Agrarian vs. Industrial. Defining the Agrarian movement as an act of intellect against itself, Tate establishes the southern movement in the Great
Critique and asserts the citizenship of its advocates in the
Republic of Letters. In his vision of this movement in the
summer of 1929—writing it will be recalled from France,
the heartland of the Third Realm—he foreshadows the
prime meaning *I'll Take My Stand* would assume as a document in American, and in a wider sense, modern history:
its implication that the literary and intellectual record of the
South is a more cogent and decisive representation of the
Third Realm than the New England record. I mean the initial representation by southern men of letters of the modern adherence to the Great Critique and its symbolization of
mind as the source and model of our history. I mean the
representation of the consequence of this in the South: the
subjectification of history and the embodiment of mind in
the self. I mean the southern representation of the struggle
in the nineteenth and twentieth centuries to transcend the
transference of mind into the self by reversing mind and society as models of history. I mean the representative effort
by southern men of letters to discover in the South as modeled on the secular-spiritual dominion of mind and art—a
dominion that, having begun in a secularization of the spiritual, awaited its transcendent fulfillment in a spiritualization of the secular. This climactic process is to be achieved
(as the "Statement of Principles" in *I'll Take My Stand* says)
by "will" and "intelligence." The necessary will and intelligence may be found (as Tate indicates here and there) in
the mild mode of Christian humanism; but although *I'll Take
My Stand* reflects an Erasmian temper at times, it flashes with
stringent and militant insights. Its chief conceivers and
instigators—the three erstwhile Fugitive poets, Ransom,

Davidson, and Tate, though not uniform in their faith, shared in common what Tate later called a "mystical secularism." They yearned, it might be said, to complete the spiritualization of the secular. By transforming the South into a symbol of a recovered society of myth and tradition, they would assert the community and spiritual authority of men of letters and make whole the fragmented realm of mind and letters.

Yet *I'll Take My Stand* is a curiously inhibited manifesto. What it proclaims as golden possibility—the reversal of mind and society—it accepts as historical impossibility. It is finally a symbol of what it basically stands against: the transference of existence into mind.

Of all the Agrarians the one most self-conscious of his descent from the exodus of the clerks, Tate burned with passion for the southern redemption of the Third Realm. His essay on the southern religion in *I'll Take My Stand* is the emblem of his passion and a redeemer's vision of the act of redeeming. In this vision Tate sees the necessity of the southern man of letters moving outside himelf to take "violent and revolutionary" political action in order "to take hold of his Tradition." Yet Tate is curiously ambivalent about the actual nature of the violence he sees as necessary. Finding the center of southern history in the Western mind's radical division between "the religious, the contemplative, the qualitative, on the one hand, and the scientific, the natural, the practical on the other," Tate appears to say that the southerner (meaning the southern writer) must in his own embodiment of mind instigate mind's rebellion against itself. In the experience of this revolutionary violence within his consciousness, the southerner will discover the South's true origin to be not mind but the old European society. But making this discovery does not lead to his incorporation in this community. The discovery is a symbol of the power of the literary imagination to establish the South as "a private, self-contained, and essentially spiritual life"; of the power of the literary mind to make a homeland for what Lionel Trilling has called the literary "secular-spiritual elect."

The deepest motive of *I'll Take My Stand* in the lives of those who had the most to do with its inception and realization was not a desire to establish a southern academy but the will to invest literary mind, as it is embodied in the individual man of letters, with the spiritual power—let me put this in the most basic way—necessary to its survival. With a certainty that southern men of letters had not known since the age of Jefferson, Ransom, Tate, Davidson, and Warren assumed that they lived within the context of the Great Critique and the Republic of Letters. Accepting this as the only possible context for the man of letters, for the poet and novelist as well as for the critic, the primary makers of the Agrarian manifesto understood that, amidst the ceaseless activity of thought that is its existence, the self of the writer establishes spiritual values for itself and other selves only by constant dedication to the awareness that consciousness is history. They understood that although existence modeled on criticism may allow more than introspection and prophecy—that although it may allow meditation—it is irrevocably closed to contemplation, and thus to the greatest source of spiritual power. Each of the primary Agrarians resisted this closure, but Tate (following his mentor T. S. Eliot) resisted it most of all. He resisted it more than Ransom, who thought that the spiritual sensibility of man might be fulfilled by making possible the purely aesthetic appreciation of the mystery and wonder exhibited by a pastoral community existing under the sovereignty of the "fairly inscrutable" Hebraic God; he resisted it more than Davidson, who was led back toward the ancient community of clan and a pagan pietas; he resisted it more than Warren, who was led toward an affirmation of the existential self within the history of the world of human beings, as this is framed by the implacable natural history of the universe.

Tate's resistance to the destruction of the contemplative mode of consciousness by the subjective mode of secular history threatened him in moments with a resignation to history not unlike that Faulkner dramatizes in Quentin Compson III, whose life was developing in Faulkner's imagination in the same period of time that *I'll Take My Stand* was in the process of conception. In a letter to John Peale Bishop in June, 1931, about a year after the publication of the Agrarian manifesto, Tate virtually is Quentin—to Faulkner a symbol of the self of the writer as a self who is not only isolated in history but who has willed the isolation of history in himself. Like Quentin, Tate (thirty-two years of age at the time of the letter) describes himself as having been at twenty older than most people who are dead. I will quote from the letter:

> . . . I think that [southern novelists] are apt to identify . . . great political and social failure with their characters, or if they are poets and concerned about themselves with their own failure. The older I get the more I realize that I set out about ten years ago to live a life of failure, to imitate, in my own life, the history of my people. For it was only in this fashion, considering the circumstances, that I could completely identify myself with them. We all have an instinct—if we are artists particularly—to live at the center of some way of life and to be borne up by its innermost significance. The significance of the Southern way of life, in my time, is failure. . . . What else is there for me but a complete acceptance of the idea of failure?

But Tate did not at the point when he expressed this sentiment to Bishop abandon the role the public reactionary.

He remained an Agrarian activist through the publication of *Who Owns America?* in 1936.

Nonetheless, turning more and more toward authoritarian Christianity, Tate concluded by 1950 that adherence to a programmatic criticism as the context of spirit is a form of heresy. He abandoned—or tried to abandon—the tactics of the Encyclopedists. A convert to Roman Catholicism, he conceived that the man of letters would render a more effective critical service to the cause of turning the society of history and science against itself when, as he said (in "The Man of Letters in the Modern World") "the cult of the literary man shall have ceased to be an idolatry." At times—may we dare suppose?—Tate dreamed of finding himself somewhere in the twelfth century in a small company of clerks; and of going about the business of the clerk, copying manuscripts and saying prayers, devoted to the vocation of waiting on the fulfillment of the Christian vision of history, as yet undisturbed by dreams of a self-willed exile in another history.

Robert B. Heilman

Spokesman and Seer: The Agrarian Movement and European Culture

I don't know how many of the participants in this conference are nonsoutherners. At any rate, it is a little difficult for one nonsoutherner not to feel like an intruder in the dust. Someone said, "Oh, you are the token Yankee." But also I was once called, in print, a "fellow-traveler of the neo-confederate party." Even at that I hardly feel like an initiate. Perhaps, then, it makes sense to accept outsidership and to approach our theme thus—as an outsider with a history that has partly affected his responses to *I'll Take My Stand*. This will mean confessing to various kinds of naïveté. If I am lucky, these may be not merely eccentric marginalia. Anyway, in this brilliant company naïveté may be the only approach not preempted by other participants.

I am of Pennsylvania German—*i.e.*, Pennsylvania Dutch—stock that, as far as our sketchy family history goes, apparently farmed the fertile rolling country of eastern Pennsylvania since mid–eighteenth century. There is no record of anyone's starving or being driven to city jobs by hard times. There is also no record of anyone's becoming a large landowner or very much of a landowner. My father's father farmed mainly but also taught all grades in a small country school. My mother's father, once a miller, was in the years I knew him a tenant farmer and a farm laborer or "hired

hand." Up into my teen years we regularly visited the Bechtolds at different country spots and had marvelous times
playing in barns and fields, riding on plow horses, feeding
chickens, gathering eggs, weeding the vegetable patch, lim-
ing the outdoor john, or stacking wood for the kitchen stove
which was usually the only source of heat in the house. My
father and his four brothers began hard farm work in very
early years; then three of them gradually worked their way
into teaching—one in local public schools, two in normal
schools. My father actually taught Greek and Latin in a normal school (today it is called, of course, a state university,
and it makes neither language available to any aspirants
there might be). Not until he was over thirty could he take
his divinity degree. During the years from my age three to
my age twelve, he was pastor of a four-church rural parish.
We lived in a town of a thousand; the parsonage was on
Main Street, but the backyard opened directly on ten miles
of open countryside that extended in a mild roll northward
to the Mahantango Mountain. From this low range, as we
watched skittishly, thunderstorms would darken the sky
and rumble ominously toward us on summer afternoons.
So life at home was only a shade less rural than we enjoyed
when visiting the Bechtolds. It too was full of joys—dam-
ming brooks, exploring creeks, taking long hikes cross country or on dirt roads, skating on frozen patches of water,
sledding on country hills after a snow, chestnut hunting on
the side of Berry Mountain just behind our town to the
south.

I make a point of these zestful pleasures because on the
whole this rural world came to seem one that could be improved on. In some unexplained way we did not think of
the scene as a permanent one. Many country people spoke
only Pennsylvania Dutch, a nonliterary German dialect;
and the English spoken was laced with Germanisms and

encrusted with German accents. The tongue could claim
no such honor as that of being an Elizabethan residue.
The classics, which we are told were standbys of agrarian
households in the South, had, as far as I know, no place
in agricultural Pennsylvania. The world of literature was
widely unknown. The country people could be very generous hosts, tables piled high with all kinds of farm produce
and pastries, but the Pennsylvania Dutch were rather well
known for a sense of the cost of things which wavered between stern prudence and severe niggardliness. Conformity in the smallest matters was taken for granted; any de-
viation in dress or speech was derided. And all the richness
of the land, which I can appreciate now more than I could at
the time, did not mitigate the strenuousness of life on the
soil. My Grandfather Bechtold's usual day was work in barn
or fields, 5 to 7; breakfast, 7 to 8; work, 8 to 12, with maybe
five minutes off somewhere for coffee; dinner, 12 to 1, with
a little rest period; then work until 6, after which he was
free for chores in his own vegetable patch, workshed, barn-
yard, or whatever. I have no recollection of his, or anyone
else's, complaining about this workday. My father and his
brothers spent a considerable number of years on such a
schedule before they managed—and I still do not see how
they managed—to make it to normal school or college.

So, despite all the genuine, indeed the passionate, pleasures of childhood play in that world of nature, country life
began to seem enclosed and a little oppressive. I do not believe that this cloudy sense of things was ever condensed
into a precise meaning that I can articulate now. Luckily we
had never heard of the word *culture*, so we could not com-
placently enroll under that banner. It was just that, in an
undefined way, better things lay elsewhere.

When I came to LSU in 1935—only the second member of
the tribe ever to live outside of Pennsylvania, and the first

to live in the South—I soon heard about *I'll Take My Stand*, and sometime in the late 1930s I did enough reading in it to get some idea of its general direction and specific proposals. I cannot recall much difficulty in ingesting revisions of the Civil War theory routinely presented to us in northern public schools, or in coming to terms with adverse criticisms of the North from mid–nineteenth century to 1930, for my filial pieties did not tend much toward regional defensiveness. Anyway, it was clear that antinorthernism was not a strict code among contributors; what came from the North was less to be rejected than to be held within limits; Tate wanted to play down the regional angle, and Warren wanted to make the book a weapon against communism. The big dose was rather the affirmative-action code: the assertion of the indispensable values of a way of life that in my experience seemed limited, constricting, and too taxing to promise much beyond a bare, hard-won subsistence. Industrialism was hardly reversible; the need seemed rather to find ways of living with it that would preserve values to which it appeared indifferent or hostile. Still, one was not ready to dismiss the agrarian credo out of hand, as I heard many southerners do. The volume came from too many gifted people to be ignored or simply rejected. I remembered the situation in Meredith's *Ordeal of Richard Feverel*, when Sir Austin explained his new educational scheme to his very common-sensical lawyer Mr. Thompson. Thompson was flabbergasted by the eccentricity of it. Still, in his view, a man who owned as many acres as Sir Austin could not be guilty of "downright folly." Similarly the writers who possessed as much intellectual acreage as was apparent in *I'll Take My Stand* could not easily be cast aside as purveyors of downright folly.

The result was some self-questioning. (It may be that the spur to questioning was a major achievement of the book;

hence, perhaps, the interest in it for many years before it was possible to do what many observers now do, that is, value it as predictive or at least prescient.) I had to ask: was there some vast fundamental difference between the agrarian life presented by the twelve southerners, and the Pennsylvania version of it? Could they speak so warmly of a life of subsistence farming because in the South that life had achieved a quality simply missing in the Pennsylvania version? They stressed the force of tradition; with us there was certainly a handed down way of life, but to the best of my knowledge it was never conceptualized or turned into an imaginative force which made the life more than the dogged repetition of inherited practices. Learning had no part in it; in Pennsylvania there was nothing of what Stark Young, with charming modesty of statement, calls "some gentlemanly acquaintance with the classics, a whiff of the poets" (349; references are to the LSU Press edition, 1977). On the other hand I did find much that was familiar in Andrew Lytle's wonderful evocation of actual daily life in the country (an evocation also partly achieved by John Donald Wade, and more thinly echoed by Henry Blue Kline). Certainly the Gemütlichkeit, if I may use that term, was something that I had known. But in the Pennsylvania scheme of things I took it to be rather the creation of especially amiable individuals than a regular accompaniment of daily life. Hence our tradition appeared to be a narrower one, stronger on the ascetic than the aesthetic. If so, were certain virtues and graces inherent in country life, or did they result from fusions of agrarian life with other influences not necessarily agrarian at all? Perhaps German country folk emigrating to Pennsylvania had never come under such influences, and so remained unamenable to them here. Not that the potential influences were totally lacking. In Pennsylvania, for example, there were some sixty colleges, most of them dating from before 1850, and from the beginnings to as late as fifty years ago serving as carriers of a classical tradition now, of course, gone down the drain. Still, they seemed to stand on the periphery of an agricultural heartland on which they had little impact. If I was correct in sensing sharp differences between the agrarianism of my ancestors and that described in *I'll Take My Stand*, was the latter then the final truth of rural life? Or a rather special product not really expectable of, or capable of being reproduced in, other parts of America? I have not answered these questions to my own satisfaction.

Another question came up: was I, without knowing it, under the influence of slogans about industry and progress? Was I, without knowing it, simply running with the times? In thinking that Pennsylvania rural life was too limited and limiting, was I undervaluing a sustaining and even satisfying element in that life? Or was I responding to various elements in the air—urbanism, mobility, jokes about rustics, fear of provincialism, advertisements plugging for an increase of comfort and ease? If I did undervalue the life I came from, this was not, I know, because I consciously responded to recognized pressures. Though I was conventional enough, I had a fairly early suspicion of going clichés, and I cannot imagine my having got addicted to the idea of progress. Even a little listening to Irving Babbitt at Harvard would have strengthened one's sense of constants not amenable to improvement by social changes. One could anticipate a continuing distribution of saints and sinners; novel systems would not notably expand grace or cut original sin.

One had two main options then. First, were there different agrarianisms that made it difficult to frame a master concept for use in social debate? Second, even in a country life that seemed deficient, were there virtues to which one was blinded by spray from the roaring stream of current history? Was one undervaluing an actual strength because of an inculcated hyperawareness of limits? But there was also a third option: that the agrarian credo was symbolic rather than programmatic, a strong base for attack by firepower rather than a homestead for year-round occupancy. As one rereads the essays now, one feels that in some of them the assertion of rural salvationary power, if not so tame as a dutiful afterthought, still lacks something of the warmth and spontaneity that almost invariably enliven the attacks on the enemy hosts. At the time, opponents liked to point out that the theorists of agrarianism were rarely practitioners of it. This line was, of course, too easy. It ignored the role of agrarianism as a symbolic force, a symbolic challenge to slogans and beliefs long unquestioned. To use the word *symbolic* resembles the approach of Louis Rubin when in 1962 he called the volume an "extended metaphor," a characterization which he was to modify in 1977. Still it has some applicability. The contributors sought a new defense for old values; the agrarian statement was a fresh way of symbolizing those values; which of course is not to say that it was exclusively symbolic. We might call the book "conditionally symbolic." We might also call it "conditionally utopian." The essays are of course admirably anti-utopian; that is, they abjure idealizations incapable of becoming incarnate in earthly sociopolitical bodies. But perhaps we can apply "utopian" to the presentation of possibilities better for humanity than the current actualities that we take for granted, and that are even puffed up by the going terms of self-esteem which every system extrudes in catchy verbal formulae. The possibilities may exist as critique rather than as pure proposals, as reminders of pursuable betterments rather than as literal designs for living. By the "utopian-symbolic" I mean the sketching of a guiding excellence somewhere between an impossible ideal and an inadequate actuality. It is this function that William Havard has in mind when he describes the consistency of the symposium with the political doctrines of Plato and Aristotle.

Given the utopian-symbolic component and the rural setting, agrarianism can easily seem an heir or mode of pastoralism. Of the invocations of the pastoral analogy that I have run into, the most interesting is the Voegelinian metaphysical analysis of the "pastoral moment" or "motive" by Lewis Simpson: the concept of Arcadia comes into being when man becomes aware of "being both a creature of the cosmos and a creature of history." Through consciousness of this symbol he seeks "redemption from history," that is, I take it, invokes permanence against change, or being against becoming (the dualism actually used by Kline, 325); or, in other terms that I have found convenient, remembers the constants as a protection against the fluid, the contingent, the relative. It is in this sense that the symposium is as much strategy as program (or what in our present fashion would doubtless be called "programmatics").

One of the only (or twinly) begetters of this conference proposed that I explore the pastoral as a source or predecessor of agrarian thought. Without prolonged research I can offer only some impressions. They have to do with literary practices rather than metaphysical implications such as Simpson deals with. Insofar as pastoral places a good life in rural scenes and occupations, it appears to be on the same wave-length as agrarianism. But the work which as far as I know comes closest to the agrarian statement is the didactic poem, Virgil's *Georgics*, which, with its faith in and rules for husbandry, seems hardly to be classified as pastoral. Virgil's *Eclogues*, deriving from the bucolic elements in Theocritus' *Idylls*, work mostly in the conventions of love and grief that

were to have a long run in Renaissance literature and to pop
up now and then in English literature for another two centuries. The fact that we can spot the conventions divides
pastoral habits from agrarian statements, which oppose the
going conventions. In general—there may be exceptions—
pastoral existed as a form of entertainment for urban or
court audiences; rather than portraying a real alternative
life, it had something of the weekend spirit; it gave a breath
of what we call "R and R," or just escape, or rustic relief.
Granted, it could contain the elegiac, which in our death-
dreading days (our major incurable disease is thanatopho-
bia), hardly seems an R-and-R theme, but the pastoral
version of this was formulaic rather than an authentic land-
grant affair. True, as in Spenser, pastoral could portray a
gallery of actual courtiers and other characters, with praise
or blame for personal and institutional ways of life, but
surely this was getting a new perspective on the familiar
rather than designing an inherently better life. For the most
part, then, pastoral exploited a pleasure in certain conventions (like the detective story in our own day) or else
achieved freshness by providing familiar experience with a
different mise-en-scène. It was less a change of life than a
change of costume, less of heart than of venue.

A third possibility derives something from both of the
first two. It appears in Lodge's *Rosalynde*, in Shakespeare's
version of it in *As You Like It*, and in a way in his *Winter's
Tale* and *Tempest*. The Forest of Arden, the Bohemian countryside, and Prospero's enchanted island are not much
more than temporary refuges. In them the innocence of
victims—victims are good by definition—has a chance to
dominate life because the bad guys, having taken over, are
all at court. Gentilesse in woods and fields is imported from
the court, and the pure natives are less likely to be country
gentlemen than risible rustics (the hick joke is one antith-

esis of the agrarian spirit). And the gentles or good guys, and dolls, are by no means wedded to their Edens; their restoration to the large world of outer affairs is the usual end of the tale. This is not the agrarian spirit.

Whether or not I am right in thinking that what separates pastoral literature and the agrarian manifesto is more conspicuous than what allies them—and obviously I am skimming surfaces rather than plumbing depths—at least this brief comparative sketch may help place agrarianism in the family of works exploring what we might call locational values.

If literary pastoralism does not offer a true model for agrarianism as a challenge to an overly worldly and busy urban life, there were actual predecessors, some with rural loyalties. Who does not think immediately of Wordsworth's "The world is too much with us . . . / Getting and spending we lay waste our powers: / Little we see in nature that is ours"? Or of his prose lament for "the increasing accumulation of men in cities, where the uniformity of their occupations produces a . . . degrading thirst after outrageous stimulation"? This came in 1800, a hundred thirty years before *I'll Take My Stand*. Or of Blake's "dark Satanic mills"? A Shelley poem describes Hell as "a city much like London." Ransom alludes both to Carlyle—we recall his scorn for the "Cash Nexus"—and to Ruskin, who inveighed against both luxury and poverty. Of the much heralded railroads Ruskin said, "Yes, now a fool can get from Guilford to Leatherhead in half an hour instead of half a day." (He anticipates Lytle's nice deflation of the clichés on time-saving: yes, "but what is to be done with this time?" [223]) In *Unto This Last* Ruskin called for "Not greater wealth, but simpler pleasure," *i.e.*, not prosperity but subsistence and plainness. Ruskin and Morris both wanted to encourage handicraft work as an alternative to machine mass production. The Aesthetic Movement of the eighties was another kind of revolt against the industrial order, though rural well-being was hardly its pitch.

Most of these protests against the industry-dominated dispensation—research would probably quadruple the record—expectably came in the nineteenth century. I find it fascinating, however, that they, and hence the Agrarians, had very vigorous predecessors in the eighteenth century, even *before* the Industrial Revolution. Sam Johnson's *London* (1738) says that the city "Sucks in the dregs of each corrupted state"; here "all are slaves to gold," and "looks are merchandise, and smiles are sold" (97, 178, 179); but a lucky man might escape to "some elegant retreat" with a view "O'er the smiling land" (212, 214). (And I can't help including a couplet of especial contemporary applicability: "Here falling houses thunder on your head, / And here a female atheist talks you dead" [17, 18].) The attack on commercial-urban evils is allied with a lament for rural decline in Goldsmith's *The Deserted Village* (1770), which paints a fairly concrete picture of village well-being that could be a sketch for Andrew Lytle's much fuller account of the plantation day. All of you will already have recalled Goldsmith's most famous couplet, "Ill fares the land, to hastening ills a prey, / Where wealth accumulates and men decay" (51–52), *i.e.*, in later idiom, "when factories multiply and men decay." Rural life was adequate: "every rood of ground" "gave what life required, but gave no more" (58, 60); but now "trade's unfeeling train / Usurp the land, and dispossess the swain" (63–64). The speaker is for "Spontaneous joys, where Nature has its play" (255). The "mournful peasant" is "scourged by famine, from the smiling land" (299, 300), and the "rural virtues leave the land" (398). He hopes that "sweet Poetry" may "Teach erring men to spurn the rage of gain" (424).

Finally, a basic line: "Thus fares the land, by luxury betray'd" (295). *Luxury* is really Goldsmith's key word for the central vice of the age. He uses it five separate times (see also 67, 283–84, 311–12, 386). What is striking about this is that it was a fundamental term of the day, denoting a concept that had a life of over two millennia, and was now a common term. Its history, as sketched in John Sekora's 1978 book, *Luxury: The Conception in Modern Thought, Eden to Smollett*, is fascinating both for the complexity of attitudes toward the idea, and for the points of contact with twentieth-century life as seen in agrarian terms. From classical and early Christian thought on, luxury was a basic term for vice, so inclusive as to be almost a synonym of "original sin" (students of literature will remember that in Tourneur's *Revenger's Tragedy* of 1607 the criminal lecher was named "Lussurioso"). The term had such polemic value that all sociopolitical combatants wanted to claim it. Established orders defined luxury as violation of "necessity and hierarchy," *i.e.*, the grasping revolutionary spirit in the lower classes. In the eighteenth century, however, luxury began to be seen, by the not-well-to-do, as the vice of the well-to-do. Again, while luxury was traditionally materialism, self-indulgence, conspicuous consumption, etc., in the eighteenth century it began, on the other hand, to be esteemed as an index of general well-being, or what we now call "prosperity"—a volte-face which obviously had to happen before modern advertising could espouse "luxury" and "luxuries" as necessities for everyman. The eighteenth century, then, was a period of transition, and Sekora has dug up numerous combatants on both sides of each of the several fences that marked the complexity of the property. He presents Tobias Smollett, especially in his novel *Humphry Clinker*, as the last major voice defending an ancient tradition. Smollett often sounds like an agrarian spokesman.

In the ancient tradition, reports Sekora, "the natural leg-
islator had been identified in the man of the land whose
birth, wealth, and intellect had elevated him to independence of other persons" (32). Cicero said, "The city creates luxury," the source of "avarice and all other crimes,"
whereas the "country life . . . teaches thrift, carefulness,
and justice" (36). For the Greeks and Romans generally,
"the model of civil polity became agrarian, paternal, and hi-
erarchical" (54). By the sixteenth century Parliament was
striving to "preserve the sanctity of the country estate" (57).
Locke was a foe, for his "redefinitions of legitimate authority seemed to cast natural law away from its ancient agrarian center" (73). John Brown's *Estimate* of 1757 "blames the
new commercial interests" "For the evils of his age" (93). A
modern English critic charges that the "British . . . were
overwhelmed by hubris after 1763. Everywhere the theme
was expansion." Sekora adds, "English victory [over France]
seemed to indicate that at least one kind of human progress, the commercial, was obtainable" (106). While Defoe
praised "tradesmen" and "manufacturers" (the word is his
[117–18]), Smollett's many volumes included the "most
sustained attack upon the luxury of the period" (136). "He
regarded the land and its resources as the ultimate economic units of a society" (137). He "boldly and vividly" por-
trayed the "ruthless, disruptive effects of unbridled com-
mercialism nearly a century before Carlyle: there can be no
doubt of Smollett's foresight into the ravages of an industrial England. No one . . . can believe Smollett exaggerated
the effects of unreformed capitalism" (138). He "indicated
that, while progress was illusory, deterioration was an accomplished fact" (141). Vulgar men take over, while "men
of true substance—'men of landed substance,' *not* 'mere
moneyed men'—go into exile or retirement" (142). *Humphry Clinker* attacks "merchants and their morality of profit,"

although one of the idea-men in the novel, Lismahago, acknowledges that "commerce is undoubtedly a blessing, while restrained within the proper channels"—an idea of a balance of elements which appears, in one way or another, in Nixon (195ff.), Warren (261, 264), Wade (284), and Kline (322). Lismahago seems to have an early idea of disastrous business cycles, anticipating Nixon, and avers that a "glut of wealth" means a "glut of evils" such as "false taste, false appetites, false wants" (224). To Smollett's gentlemen, Sekora sums up, "luxury is a many-sided threat. With its vulgarity and prostitution luxury undermines grace, hospitality, and fine manners" (287).

Surely the language of these quotations makes clear enough the parallels between luxury-thought and the agrarian thought of almost two centuries later. Two agrarian obiter dicta use the eighteenth-century key term: Lytle's that "if he [the "money-crop" farmer] makes any money, it goes for luxuries instead of discharging his debt" (240), and Lanier's on the farmer's being "kept in poverty" by the "purchase of needless luxuries" made seductive by advertising (152).

Finally, it is fascinating to see how, in Smollett's scheme of things, Scotland plays American South to London's and England's American North. I quote: "London's demands for luxury are so voracious that it despoils the remainder of the nation" (277), and, "as London is plundering the rest of England, so England is plundering Scotland." A visitor to Scotland asserts, "I have met with more kindness, hospitality, and rational entertainment, in a few weeks, than ever I received in any other country during the whole course of my life" (278). All agree that Scotland "represents a better because *older* way of living. Refusing to bend to the blasts of fashion to the south, the people and their institutions have kept fast the best of ancient traditions, remaining hardy and virile" (280). Sekora summarizes: "Smollett's vision of genuine worth did not project an *alternative* society. . . . Rather he posited the value of an *earlier* society—one where life was simpler and where order, station, and identity were firmly established and respected" (286).

Needless to say, this notation of parallels is neither the literary game of source hunting nor a way of alleging that agrarian thought is derivative. Rather it underlines the durability of certain concepts. *I'll Take My Stand* clearly belongs to a strong, nonlocalized tradition of dissent against the commercial, and then the industrial, dogma of well-being. This continuity is impressive in itself. But it is more than impressive. The long life of the value patterns espoused in agrarian thought is evidence of their deep-rootedness, and surely it is this that accounts for the predictiveness or prescience which has been widely attributed to the 1930 volume. You have to start very deep if you're going to have a lookout high enough to let you see very far. Too, the deeper the roots, the greater the strength for a battle essential in every culture. I mean the attack on the clichés which, in our media-dominated world, are the chief currency of thought and are therefore likely to seem endowed with metaphysical validity. My sense of things is that the cliché of progress (cf. Young, 343) has been superseded by the clichés of change (that is, all change is necessarily beneficent) and of mobility as inherently advantageous; and the cliché of prosperity by the cliché of socialism. Of course agrarianism had attacked the cliché of socialism fifty years ago, and at least inferentially the clichés of change and mobility.

Among the statements which have the dual role of undermining a cliché and affirming an alternative, the one of greatest resonance, I believe, is John Ransom's challenge of the view that our "destiny" is "to wage an unrelenting war on nature" and to "conquer nature," and his balancing assertion that man's true course is to work out "a truce with nature," so that "he and nature seem to live on terms of mutual respect and amity" (7). Back in the thirties this struck me immediately as both fresh and enlightening, and I never forgot the idea. Returning to the volume this year, I noted the echo of Ransom's thought in other essays. I have not time to quote, as I should like to do, but there are statements about the value to human beings of contact with nature, with earth, with land, with soil in the essays by Davidson, Owsley, Lanier (in that fine roll-call of the philosophical generators of the idea of progress), Lytle, Wade, and Young, who sums up the matter when he refers to "the form of labor in which the mystery and the drama of life— the seed, the flower and harvest, the darkness, the renewal—is most represented to us" (347). But Ransom's word *truce* is the key. You make truces only with doughty and worthy foes. Since nature is indeed a doughty foe, one misses, in the symposium, the consistent acknowledgment of the sheer difficulty and often hardship of farming life. Davidson and Tate make passing references to the hostility of nature, but only Lytle, who had firsthand knowledge, seems regularly aware of nature as a tough customer, as both "destroyer and preserver," if I may quote a not very fashionable poet. Then there is the nature of the preservative action, which is also left implicit. Obviously it is more than subsistence. One implication is that subsisting on the soil produces the human society of most worth, one that unites its members in a common cause lived rather than lobbied. Beyond subsistence and society there is also, it is implied, a sustenance of a nonmaterial or spiritual sort.

One is tempted to use the word *mystical*. But that might mislead, suggesting Wordsworth or Blake—nature as affording an epiphany of truth or a symbol of ultimate reality. In agrarian thought, however, the earth is rather a transrational communicator of moral or psychic well-being for which there is no other source.

If I am right in reading in these essays a faith in the beneficent impact of soil on soul—I bypass the large issue of ownership, of whether soil profits if it is not property, and whether as property it produces a good beyond property—then I have to wonder where we are now, when agriculture has become mainly an industry, and the man-land relationship of subsistence is, for individuals, families, and communities, much rarer than it was fifty years ago. Have we lost an ingredient essential to an adequate way of life? Does an unspoken sense of that loss inspire a reversal of a two-hundred-year trend—the reversal which we call, probably hyperbolically, the flight from the cities? The creation of "green belts" in urban areas? Living in outlying or rural areas that require long commuting trips for urban workers? Keeping small secondary homes, cottages mostly, at shore or in mountains? Amateur efforts at vegetable gardening? The more frequent efforts at flower gardening? Even the more recent architectural trick which puts green belts inside houses? Apparently we assume that, if we can't have two feet always on the ground, it is a good thing to be knuckle deep in dirt now and then. Is this our simulacrum of a truce with nature? If it is a fake, we are in a bad way. We may have to look with new seriousness at Oswald Spengler's dictum of 1918 that when man leaves the land, culture gives way to civilization and a chaotic way of life. And on the other side of the fence our recurrent urban brownouts (or blackouts) give a new substance to E. M. Forster's famous image of impending disaster for modern life, his short story "The Machine Stops." Its date was, fascinatingly enough, 1928.

Perhaps the greatest success of the book is that it makes us think about such problems. It bucked the clichés of its day. While undermining clichés, it posed counter values, as a critic must. At the same time it evaded the risk of falling into a simple melodrama of good and evil. The dominant theme is less "Chicago delenda est" than a balance of various regional values and of socioeconomic modes. The book lauds a traditional agrarian life without falling into the simplistic dogma of farmer Dagley in *Middlemarch*; Eliot alludes to his "farming conservatism, which consisted in holding that whatever is, is bad, and any change is likely to be worse" (Ch. 39).

Now the challenging of clichés without simply putting out a nest egg of counter clichés or anti-clichés means a kind of general perceptiveness which pervades, underlies, and even stands apart from immediate polemic sorties. Many passages invite one, as it were, to take them out of context, for they are neither liberty turned crotchety, nor old saws dulled by overuse. Such passages are self-updating, that is, so rooted in cultural and moral realities as to survive for half a century and help upset our own tool-kit of handy clichés. They reveal a moral core that, uneroded by fashions, gave the program itself, whatever its literal feasibility, a strong claim to continuing attention and respect.

Sometimes the passages are aphoristic or apothegmatic. While the book defends leisure against a hyperkinetic busyness, and deplores a leisure become "feverish and energetic" (Davidson, 34), it also insists, rightly, both that an indefinite reduction of "labor-time" means "satiety and aimlessness" and that "the act of labor [is] one of the happy functions of human life" (Introduction, xlii, xli). Thus it counters a tedious cliché of our own day: the always shrill abuse of the "Protestant work ethic" (an ethic articulated, unless my history of ideas is hopelessly skewed, not in the Reformation but in the *Nicomachean Ethics*). The clichés that literally rule educational practice today were deflated fifty years ago. Take the cliché that democratic education must be infinitely adjusted to all comers, like goods in a department store to all shoppers. Fletcher exactly describes our situation: the "unlimited range of disconnected subjects, all open as possible 'credits,' and the same lack of an organic curriculum" (116). Beyond that, the more fundamental cliché that education can do everything with and for men. As Lanier puts it, "Man is not a *tabula rasa* on which arbitrary patterns may be inscribed without regard to his natural propensities" (142), and, as Fletcher puts it, even more absolutely, "All that education can do in any case is to teach us to make good use of what we are; if we are nothing to begin with, no amount of education can do us any good" (93).

On art: Davidson criticizes the Imagists as romantics whose "art is exclamatory and personal [and] avoids synthesis and meaning" (45), and Kline rebukes artists who engage in "fruitless contemplation of their own beings" (312). Thus both reject the cliché of the artist as hemmed-in solitary whose subjectivity is his only resource, and hence that more general malaise of the 1970s that we now know as "narcissism." Too, Kline denies that the "purpose of art [is] to show the purposelessness of everything outside one's own ego" (312) and declares the public airing of "pessimistic views" to be the "most shocking kind . . . of spiritual immodesty" (314). Aside from spotting proclaimed despair as a self-displaying on street corners, Kline catches long in advance a cliché so assimilable that it came to be rattled off by undergraduates everywhere—the cliché of absurdist existentialism. I think it fair to say that with us the word *rights* has become a cliché, that is, an unexamined slogan word applied indiscriminately to all sorts of desires. As Wade says of a critic of Cousin Lucius, "that bounding youngster . . . wanted, without effort, things that have immemorially come as the result of effort only" (292). As for deserts and rights, Wade makes a subtle discrimination that we rarely hear: "The practice of a perfectly sound 'right' often involves the practicer, and with him others, in woes incomparably more galling than the renunciation of that right" (289). Kline puts a finger on another kind of self-indulgence, that of "self-torturers . . . romantic idealists disillusioned by the sharp prick of reality, defeated by the unideal conditions of sensuous existence . . . wish[ing] not to shape a satisfactory environment but to escape the effort of adjusting themselves to any sort of conditions whatever" (307). Thus they become, one might add, set-ups for the spiritual pigeon-drops of communism, communes, and instant communions cadged up by christomimetic fast-buck artists and self-deceiving charisma-peddlers.

The rigidity that rejects the going, imperfect world creates another cliché, the cliché of "sincerity" as absolute virtue. Young cuts sharply into this masquerade: "Such forms of sincerity are usually ill-bred egotism" (346), "a sincerity that consists of boorishness and peasant egotism" (337), and it is only "self-centered boors" who reject routine courtesies (346). Young's definition of bad manners has much use for us now. Besides, he combines the case for manners with the case for a true independence of judgment and spirit. This independence invariably bows to the rites of social intercourse, but does not bow to the pressures of popular opinion. "Politicians may flatter the masses. But the ignorant do not possess every man of any intelligence, who should love and despise rather than indulge them; . . . there will never again be distinction in the South [or anywhere else, I might add] until—somewhat contrary to the doctrines of popular and profitable democracy—it is generally clear that no man worth anything is possessed by the people, or sees the world under the smear of the people's wills or beliefs" (338). In a day when polls make policy, elections establish excellence, and the media mob the man in the street to mine his meditations on all matters, Young's antipopulist caveat should be broadcast daily.

Young boldly calls essential social virtues "aristocratic." Actually, he defines the word in a way that makes the quality available to all who will diligently court it. But courting it would mean, right now, having to resist several popular cliché attitudes. Aristocracy means, Young says, "an innate code of obligations"—obligations, not "rights." It means "self-control"—"self-control," not letting fly, in the name of freedom, with every random lust. Self-control "implied not the expression of you and your precious personality" (discipline, not the "self-expression" that our age takes for granted as a need and indeed a right), and not "the pleasures of suffering or denying your own will" (that is, of masochism). Rather, Young goes on, "you controlled yourself in order to make the society you lived in more decent, affable, and civilized, and yourself more amenable and attractive" (350). Put these passages together, and you have the happy union of a thorough independence that does not degenerate into a privateering willfulness or self-proclamation, with a social sense and style that acknowledge the claims and existence of others. It joins a proper pride and a proper humility: freedom from others' minds, but subservience to their social comfort and pleasure. That is an aristocratic condition open to the earning. It undermines another modern cliché: the anti-elitism which is an increasingly serious danger to our culture. Anti-elitism is that egalitarianism in which a mask of distaste for unearned privilege hides a genuine dislike of earned excellence, not to mention native superiority. Young spots that failing too. In deploring a debased Puritan "whining on certain pious excellences," he attributes it in part to "a half-conscious jealousy of all distinction" (377). With us, that quiet under-the-skin motive can become a real curse. For anti-elitism is self-promotion, which figures in two other current clichés: hypertrophy of the accusatory instinct, and hypertrophy of discontent with human vulnerability.

The South condensed in *I'll Take My Stand* was to enjoy a victory—not indeed the victory of formal doctrine over social practice, but still the achievement of an end that is always voiced in the text, implicitly and sometimes explicitly. That end is the creation of morale, of a sense of regional worth which would eliminate vulnerability to condescensions from elsewhere. It was, if you will, the Trojan mode of triumph—another Aeneas, Anchises on his back, going forth from the ashes to help shape a new order. The ultimate victory was probably not foreseen in 1930. It was the victory of a literary flowering unequaled, I believe, by any other regional phenomenon of letters in this country. But if "unforeseen" in 1930, still not wholly unguessed at. I have in mind a modest statement by Davidson: "I do not suggest that the South is about to become the seat of some great revival of the arts—though such might happen. I do suggest that the South, as a distinct, provincial region, offers terms of life favorable to the arts" (56–57). Well, the creators of literary arts were, and are, there.

In this there is something of the sheer grace of the goddess Fortuna: there is no rational accounting for a bumper crop of raw talent, and then one crop after another. There comes to mind, also, Young's fine statement, that "the greatest, most luminous defense of any point of view is its noble embodiment in persons" (334). There have been some noble embodiments—obviously among the symposiasts themselves, and impressively in the crops of writers coming up steadily ever since. Still, such crops are never ripened by doctrine. "Point of view," Young's term, must mean less dogma than insight. The apologist must metamorphose into the free historian and the humanist who is at once synoptic and deep-digging. How brought about? Who knows? I suspect that the nourishing soil is a contact with literal soil, but with soil that is also a place. It is a place with a meaning, a meaning, as Wordsworth put it, "Felt in the blood, and felt along the heart." The place is at once the provider of a concrete scene and an anchor of feeling; yet the writer's grasp of the concrete is allied with a reflectiveness which has, as it must, its own abstractions; and the place-bound stability of feeling, though never displaced, is modified by a mobility that brings in, as a source of creative tension, the stimulus of absence of and memory, and something of an altered sensibility. Loyalty is yoked to a separateness whereby, though one is of this place, one is not wholly tied to it; attachment is conjoined with a detachment that helps transform the spokesman into the seer.

And these words, I think, explain the longevity of the agrarian manifesto: in the end the spokesman—the chosen, public role—is a lesser figure than the not so visible center of force, the seer. And in the literary flowering that came after, the spokesman faded away in the seer.

Agrarianism, Criticism, and the Academy

Ford Madox Ford observed that the artist cannot be a gentleman. As students of the South and the modern world we cannot ignore this dictum, for Ford's obsession with the idea and ideal of the gentleman has emblematic significance. Ford tells us that after his bank mistakenly dishonored several of his checks he was no longer a gentleman. In view of his bizarre marital arrangements for some years previous, this conclusion on Ford's part seems more than a little comical and quixotic. It was Ezra Pound, whom nobody ever mistook for a gentleman, who said that he could leave Ford naked and alone in a locked empty room and come back an hour later to find chaos. If we search for a modern artist who is also a gentleman, we might have to look for a long time in certain quarters. Among the great modernists perhaps only T. S. Eliot would qualify.

Whether or not the artist is a gentleman in the true sense—and God knows that he seldom qualifies—he brings chaos in his wake; and the writer is more notorious in this way than perhaps any other kind of artist. "As a class," Malcolm Cowley has observed, writers "have distinguished themselves as barroom brawlers, drawing-room wolves, breakers of engagements, defaulters of debts, crying drunks, and suicidal maniacs." In the circumstances the administrator in a given college or university—the president, dean, or department head—has every reason to be chary of the breed. There is a certain natural antagonism between the academic world and the community of letters not only because art has an uncomfortable way of embodying the unpleasant respects of reality and bringing the reader to the edge of the abyss but because the artist in his personal life has a shocking inclination to jump cheerfully into the abyss, attempting to drag the mere middleman or bystander, no doubt an innocent and virtuous chap—let us say the dean—with him.

I bring up this subject by way of examining the uneasy relation between the Fugitives and Agrarians and the university, especially Vanderbilt University. If the writers in question had been the kind of people that artists frequently are so far as their personal lives and habits are concerned, one could be more sympathetic to the fashion in which they were often treated by the administration at Vanderbilt. One of the ironies of this relation and its intricate web of complementary connections is that these men were almost without exception models of decorum. John Crowe Ransom was the quintessential gentleman, a man who used manners as a mask and a shield and a man whose self-control was almost invariably perfect. Most of the writers with whom the Fugitives and Agrarians were associated were also mannerly, decent people. The exceptions—the Hart Cranes, Laura Ridings, Hemingways, etc.—had little or no bearing on the university's relation with its own writers. In short Vanderbilt had little of which to complain. It got superior teaching and superior publications from this group—as faculty members and as students and, later, as alumni. (Sometimes the faculty members were alumni, needless to say.)

That the relation was uneasy is logical, however, despite the orderly lives of most of the Fugitives and Agrarians.

The university is naturally suspicious of the artist, and in the early days of this century the artist had not yet found a home in the university. He could expect little or nothing of the private patron or of his publisher; literary agents were few and far between; and the foundation was a fledgling enterprise. (Tate received one of the first Guggenheim fellowships in 1928.) For the leading Fugitives and Agrarians—Ransom, Davidson, Tate, Lytle, and Warren—writing was a vocation; in contrast, being on the faculty of a university was chiefly a means of making a living. In fact it was the best and most natural way of satisfying the requirements of the mundane and contingent world, and for the most part these men spent their careers associated with the academy. Of them only Warren had the talent, drive, and temperament to be a full-time professional writer; and only Tate aside from Warren tried to be a free-lance writer for long periods of time. In the sense of making a decent living Tate was unsuccessful as a writer.

The other vocation that these men might have naturally taken up is journalism, and although some of them—principally Ransom—thought seriously of being journalists, and all of them thought more seriously still of starting a newspaper and a popular magazine, none became a journalist. Temperamentally all were far more suited to the university than to the city room, and none could have said, as did H. G. Wells: "I had rather be called a journalist than an artist, that is the essence of it." (One can be doubly sure that none of these writers would have made that remark to Henry James.) Although they occasionally wrote for such magazines as the *Saturday Review, Harper's,* and the *Atlantic Monthly,* it is clear that they would not have been comfortable as staff writers for such magazines or even for the *New Yorker.* Just as one cannot imagine Edmund Wilson teaching English or comparative literature or even advanced writing at a university, he cannot envision Tate or Warren working regularly as editor or author for the *New Yorker*, even though the natural antipathy between the profession of letters and journalism is probably less than the friction between the profession of letters and the teaching profession, not to mention the administration that supports and directs the faculty of any university. Journalism provided a home and a training ground for many of the best writers in this country until the recent past, and until mid-century it was far more important in this regard than was the university. One immediately thinks of Hemingway, Bernard DeVoto, Malcolm Cowley, Thurber, E. B. White, Joseph Mitchell, A. J. Liebling, H. L. Mencken, Edmund Wilson, and others; but this avenue has generally not appealed to writers from the South, in or out of the academy. The university-educated writer, particularly the writer with graduate work behind him, has tended to gravitate to the academy; the journalist, even a man so well-educated as Liebling, has in contrast used the newspaper beat as his university. Writers of this stripe, including ones as sophisticated as Liebling and Wilson, are inclined to take a dim view of the academic world. Liebling called the Lost Generation "monkeys on a raft," and he regularly used to twit "the boys on the literary quarterlies" who habitually use such academic expressions as *dichotomy* and *frame of reference*.

But I must give the academy—Vanderbilt, Louisiana State University, the University of North Carolina (especially the Women's College), Princeton, and other schools—its due. Often the academy was not so much unfriendly to writers in general and the Fugitives and Agrarians in particular as it was indifferent to them. If we get down to specific hard cases and discuss men like Chancellor James H. Kirkland and Professor Edwin Mims, we see that Kirkland signed a note for Ransom to support his sabbatical leave in England

and that Mims had Ransom promoted on much the same basis as a properly academic scholar, Walter Clyde Curry, was promoted. Randall Stewart pointed out this admirable fact about Mims long ago in "The Relation Between Fugitives and Agrarians." The old man did not want to be remembered as he will be remembered—as the chap who tried to prevent the publication of the *Fugitive*, who blocked Tate's appointment to graduate study, who did not promote and retain Warren, who regularly thwarted and frustrated Davidson, and who, above all, let Ransom go to Kenyon.

No man has ever waxed more lyrical over the advantages of Old High Germanic graduate education than did Mims, and no man has ever held the simple and simpleminded fact of having a Ph.D. so dear. Mims never let Ransom, Davidson, and the rest forget that they had not reached such olympian heights, and for mysterious reasons (which probably included good manners) each of them let the autocratic chairman get away with his academic balderdash. Needless to say, Ransom, Davidson, Tate, and Warren, not to mention Lytle, Brooks, and others, are among the best educated writers of their time or any time and were not only better read and more intelligent but better educated than most of their colleagues in the university, not excluding the redoubtable Dr. Mims. As his letters clearly show, Ransom always was defensive about not getting a Ph.D., and at one time he planned to go to Harvard for graduate study. Fortunately he never got around to it. Tate, being brash and aggressive, never let his lack of graduate education bother him very much; but he flaunted a Phi Beta Kappa key by way of compensation. All his mature life Davidson squirmed about not having a Ph.D., even though he knew that the degree amounted to very little; and he could have said with as much or more justice what Kittredge did at Harvard about his lack of a Ph.D.: "Who would examine me?"

Since these men began their associations with the university when there was not a comfortable berth in the university for a writer, they were often treated as second-class citizens. Ironically enough it was Tate who was appointed as the first writer-in-residence; but the appointment was at Princeton, not Vanderbilt. Immediately prior to that appointment in 1939 he was at the Women's College in Greensboro, North Carolina, serving, he said, as "a publicized idler, or a dray-horse advertised as a race-horse." He went to Princeton to teach writing. Only a little earlier Ransom had achieved similar recognition when he became professor of poetry at Kenyon College. Davidson never was given special status at Vanderbilt for his ability as a writer; Warren was properly recognized only after leaving the South.

The academy, especially in the South, was less an alma mater, a fostering mother, to the Fugitives and Agrarians than it was an irritant. (I am not speaking of their relation to the academy as students, of course, but as faculty members.) True-blue academicism stuck so deeply in the craws of these men that none of them ever quite managed to rid himself of this irritant. The irritant was salutary, however: it proved to be the grain of sand in the oyster's craw, and it produced more than one pearl.

If, gentle reader, you are wondering what in God's name my comments on the behavior of the artist, the grave rites and courtesies of the Nashville group, and the expectations of the university administration have to do with Agrarianism and criticism, let me say that I have not forgotten my subject and am warming to it. But I am approaching it warily. The beginning is in sight.

Anyone, no matter how unfriendly and benighted—even a John L. Stewart or Alexander Karanikas—who survey the individual and collective careers of the leading Fugitives and Agrarians will see a common thread which runs through their work from beginning to end—the commitment to poetry. As Warren has said, for the Fugitives "poetry was all." They were writers first, especially poets, and then biographers, historians, classicists, polemicists, fictionists, teachers, and critics. First and foremost was the commitment to poetry and to all that commitment entails, especially to what Lewis P. Simpson deems the Republic of Letters. (Although Ransom said life must come first, Tate made it plain throughout his long career as a man of letters that his first loyalty was to the Fourth Estate and that family and friends and other entanglements in the mundane world were matters of lesser import and could be discounted accordingly.) It was Davidson, the most committed of the Agrarians in both an ideological and a practical sense, who observed to Tate about Agrarianism: "We are, after all, writers before everything else—and only secondarily, if at all, cavalry commanders, orators, lobbyists, and ward-heelers." He went on to say: "We ought to write, then, and keep writing, as we have done in the past, with the sure conviction that if our ideas are right, we shall in the end reach the people who can do the other needful things." The same kind of conviction applies in general to their other campaigns within and without the academy.

If we look hastily at their various commitments, we see that the Fugitives began talking about philosophy but rapidly switched to poetry and that the commitment to poetry led in turn to the founding of the *Fugitive* magazine, which had a brilliant but short run. As Tate has pointed out, it was one of the few magazines of its kind to founder for lack of an editor rather than lack of money; by 1925 the Fugitives were all too busy writing to let editing interfere with their work. But all of the principals returned to editing of one kind and another, of course: Davidson to his book page in the Nashville *Tennessean* in 1930, Warren (with Brooks) to the first series of the *Southern Review* in 1935, Ransom to the *Kenyon Review* in 1939, and Tate to the *Sewanee Review* in 1944. Of great significance in the context of my argument is that many of them edited college textbooks, beginning in the late 1930s, especially Brooks and Warren with *Understanding Poetry*.

The interest in philosophy, needless to say, did not lead to much, if anything, that would qualify as philosophy pure and simple; but the criticism of Ransom, who read philosophy at Christ Church, Oxford, as a Rhodes scholar, and of Tate, who somehow read himself into a wide knowledge of philosophy, often has a dense philosophical texture, as does *God Without Thunder*; and Warren is a philosophical novelist and poet, as has often been observed.

Next came the engagement with history, which led in large part to the writing of biography—Warren's *John Brown: The Making of a Martyr* (1929), Tate's *Stonewall Jackson* (1928) and his *Jefferson Davis* (1929), Lytle's *Bedford Forrest and His Critter Company* (1931), and Davidson's two-volume history of the Tennessee River (1946, 1948). This is a subject that has been scanted in the various books and essays on the Fugitives and Agrarians. Tate said in conversation that Davidson was more nearly a historian than a man of letters or a professor of English; and Warren's lifelong love of history can be seen throughout his career, most recently in his *New Yorker* essay on Jefferson Davis and in his interview in *U.S. News and World Report*.

The interest in classics was also lifelong with most of the leading Agrarians. Any one of them might have forged a distinguished career as a classical scholar, especially Ransom; and one remembers Tate's translations. Lillian Feder has demonstrated the importance of the classics in Tate's poetry; and Ward Allen has done the same for Davidson's.

Agrarianism combined some of these interests, especially that in history, with interests in other matters, particularly economics, sociology, and religion. Of course there was the general loyalty to the South, which became intensified in consequence of the South's rejoining the country after World War I and its feeling the cultural shock of the modern world and of the attacks on the South by Mencken and others, especially in connection with the Scopes trial at Dayton in 1925. The leading Agrarians investigated certain subjects in connection with the symposium, chiefly economics; and we recollect Ransom's homemade studies in economics which he pursued in England. The sociological bent can be seen in many of the essays that were contributed by the Agrarians to the *American Review* and in Davidson's *Attack on Leviathan*. As Davidson said in 1952, the religious dimension was neglected—except in Tate's essay.

The success of Agrarianism is ideological, not practical, as should have been evident from the beginning. That the work of the Agrarians—especially *I'll Take My Stand*—has a continuing value and impact is obviously a donnée not only of this but of other recent celebrations of the fiftieth anniversary of the book's publication. One can argue that the comparative failure of the Agrarian movement on the political plane was caused not so much by the attacks of their opponents and the indifference of the great mass of the American public but by the Agrarians' own increasing boredom with that particular subject. That was especially true of Ransom, and in September of 1936 he wrote to Tate: "What is true in part for you (though a part that is ominously increasing) is true nearly in full for me: *patriotism* has nearly eaten me up, and I've got to get out of it." In leaving Vanderbilt Ransom divested himself not only of Kirkland and Mims but of Agrarianism and patriotism, as Thomas Daniel Young has made clear in his biography of Ransom.

By that same year, 1936, when the second Agrarian symposium, *Who Owns America?*, had been published, Agrarianism as a movement was rapidly ending. The *American Review* had ceased publication; Brooks and Warren were immersed in the *Southern Review*; Tate was at Southwestern; Ransom would soon be at Kenyon. The Agrarians were returning to the academy, especially to the classroom, and to the community of letters; and hereafter they would have little to do with garden-variety politics. By this time many of them were living outside the South; and Richard Weaver called this condition "Agrarianism in exile," in an essay of the same title.

Grant Webster, in a perversely ingenious and usually wrong-headed book entitled *The Republic of Letters*, has said in a piece of comical hyperbole that the Agrarians, having failed to take over the country, decided to take over the academy instead. Webster has a point: the New Criticism established a hegemony in the American university in the 1940s and 50s that was broken only fairly recently, and it is amusing to see how often the critics who say that the New Criticism is dead prop up the dead bodies which presumably litter the stage of literary history and launch still another frontal assault. Reports of the death of the New Criticism, like the early reports of Mark Twain's death, have been greatly exaggerated. One of the ironies of the current literary and critical scene, in and out of the academy, is that the stock of Agrarianism continues to rise while the New Criticism is being battered on all sides, often by people who are closer to being New Critics than they realize or would care to admit.

But I am getting ahead of the story. My fundamental point at this juncture is simple: the Agrarians, who by this time included Brooks as well as Ransom, Davidson, Tate, Warren, and Lytle, now turned their enormous energy and talent not only into writing literature—the late thirties saw the publication of Lytle's *The Long Night*, Ransom's Phi Beta Kappa poem, "Address to the Scholars of New England," Warren's *Night Rider*, and Tate's *The Fathers*—but also into the forging of a criticism that was at once a new way of looking at literature, especially the literature of modernism, and a new way of teaching literature. So there is a conjunction of critical studies—Brooks's *Modern Poetry and the Tradition*, Ransom's *The World's Body* and *The New Criticism*, Tate's *Reactionary Essays* and *Reason in Madness*—with textbooks, especially *Understanding Poetry*. Brooks and Warren had already edited *An Introduction to Literature*, and would soon add *Understanding Fiction* to their textbooks. We should also remember Davidson's *American Composition and Rhetoric*; Ransom's *Topics for Freshman Writing* and *A College Primer of Writing*; and finally Tate and Caroline Gordon's *The House of Fiction*. By the time *The House of Fiction* was published in 1950, the New Criticism was dominant in and out of the academy; the only wholly new textbook that any of these men has edited since that time is *American Literature: The Makers and the Making*, which Brooks and Warren edited with R. W. B. Lewis and which was published in 1974. This two-volume anthology represents the New Criticism for the classroom in a new phase, buttressed by biography, literary history, and social and intellectual history. Behind it one sees Brooks's history of literary criticism and his two-volume work on Faulkner, just as he sees the complementary relation of *Modern Poetry and the Tradition* and *The Well Wrought Urn* to *Understanding Poetry*.

By the end of the Agrarian movement only Davidson's career might be said to have crested. After 1938 when his best book, *The Attack on Leviathan*, was published, he spent much of his energy writing essays in an embattled and lonely defense of Agrarianism (and the Old South) and in writing and editing textbooks. With the exception of his fine late poems and his history of the Tennessee River this accounts for the great bulk of his published work after 1938. In any case his literary criticism is of a different kind and order from that of the others and is less central to his writing and to his thought. This largely results from Davidson's having a different view of the springs of literature from the others. Davidson sees the proper role of the poet as prophet, bard, and minstrel; Ransom, Tate, Warren, and the others view him in his modern role as the alienated clerk. (I am here following Lewis Simpson once again.) Davidson would not have thought of the artist as properly part of a third or fourth estate which is alienated from church and state and from society. Davidson's increasing sense of loneliness and isolation was counterproductive, for he needed the sense of a community to uphold and sustain him. Patriotism continued to gnaw at his vitals long after Ransom had rejected Agrarianism and the others had become indifferent to it.

To say that Ransom, Tate, and Warren simply transferred their energy from Agrarianism to the New Criticism is simplistic at best, and it denies what one knows not only of these men but of artists in general. It is easy to do violence to the relationship of their commitment to poetry on the one hand—by which I mean literature in the broad sense, especially poetry and fiction—and criticism on the other. It is fairly evident that they were wearied by the Agrarian campaigns and frustrated by their lack of success in an immediate practical sense. But there were other elements in solution, none of which might be called the catalyst but each of which possessed catalytic properties. Ransom, although not a leader in the ordinary sense of the term, was the man to whom the others looked; and in the middle thirties Ransom turned to criticism with great relish and zest, making it his chief occupation for the remainder of his life. Literary theory had interested Ransom from the time that he was a Rhodes scholar at Oxford; now having long since lost interest in writing poetry and in being an Agrarian and an amateur economist, he began writing the best and most characteristic of his critical essays. Tate was not far behind, and Brooks, as Tate said in one of the last critical pieces that he wrote, soon provided "a synthesis of the critical works of I. A. Richards, T. S. Eliot, John Crowe Ransom, and, to a small extent, myself." When he wrote *Modern Poetry and the Tradition* criticism had come of age, and American critics were just as good or better than their counterparts in England—Eliot, Richards, Empson, Leavis, and other writers associated with *Scrutiny*. The leading Agrarians wrote criticism not only in a positive response to Eliot and the others but in a negative reaction against Marxism and Marxist criticism (one remembers the alternative title that was proposed for *I'll Take My Stand—Tracts Against Communism*) and against the New Humanism of Irving Babbitt, Paul Elmer More, and others, not to mention the historical scholarship of R. S. Crane, Douglas Bush, A. O. Lovejoy, *et al*.

The work that Brooks and Warren did on the *Southern Review* naturally whetted their own critical appetites, especially Brooks's; and anyone who reads the first series of the *Southern Review*, the *Kenyon Review* in the forties and fifties, and the *Sewanee Review* under Lytle and Tate in the mid-forties and later under John Palmer and Monroe Spears can see the critical campaigns that were regularly waged. My point is that the rise of the New Criticism, southern style, was almost inevitable, given this combination of circumstances. Criticism possessed excitement and style and vitality, and it is worth noting that R. S. Crane obviously felt left out and turned from old-fashioned historicism to inventing neo-Aristotelianism as he fought with Ransom and the other southerners.

At the same time these men were much involved in the affairs of the academy: Ransom went to the Rockefeller Foundation with Gordon Chalmers, president of Kenyon, and came away with funds to support *Kenyon Review* fellowships and the Kenyon School of English, not to mention paying the quarterly's contributors on a higher scale. Brooks and Warren were involved in efforts to get a good president for LSU and a good chairman of the English department; Tate tried to get Ransom to move to Greensboro and become the chairman of the English department at the Women's College and almost succeeded; and so forth. Some of these endeavors fell short of success, as Robert Heilman will confirm about LSU. He and Brooks went to visit the president of LSU's board of supervisors in a fruitless attempt to block the appointment of the old warhorse who in time became the university president. The worthy president of the board, according to Heilman, "made honest use of a good thing, or took a deadpan demonic revenge" on the two young critics by presenting not only the poetry of his wife but the good woman herself. Neither the document nor its maker passed the test on literary grounds, needless to say. The old warhorse was appointed despite the heroic efforts of Heilman and Brooks at the presidential and Pierian springs; and soon thereafter the general, in a burst of patriotic effort doubtless calculated to shorten the war, suspended publication of the *Southern Review*. He doubtless also had the backing of the old boys of the faculty, some of whom Warren would later describe as "torpid as an alligator in the cold mud of January" and others as "avid to lick the spit of an indifferent or corrupt administration." In 1942 the first series of the *Southern Review* ended, and Warren left for the University of Minnesota; he would later join Brooks at Yale in 1950. In 1951 Tate took Warren's place at Minnesota. Earlier he had been forced to resign from the editorship of the *Sewanee Review*. By 1947, when Brooks left LSU for Yale, the southern academy had almost purged itself of the Agrarians. There was nothing deliberate about this purging, which occurred mainly through ignorance, indifference, and resistance to change.

Earlier in the decade another series of events occurred which showed what Thomas Daniel Young has called "the Vanderbilt administration's equivocal and disparaging attitude toward the Fugitives and Agrarians" when it all but refused to accept Davidson and Tate's papers as a gift. Princeton promptly bought Tate's for $70,000. Over a decade would pass before Vanderbilt would officially recognize the Fugitives with the reunion of 1956. And many more years would pass before the Wills collection would be established in the Joint University Library.

In the meanwhile none of these men—Davidson excepted—was fretting much about his position vis-à-vis the academy. Tate was writing some of the best criticism of his long career, as were Ransom and Brooks; and Warren was writing not only superb criticism but some of his best poetry and fiction. The *Kenyon* and *Sewanee* reviews were publishing a good deal of this work. By 1946, when *All the King's Men* was published, the first and most important phase of the southern renascence was over; and the New Criticism, which depended very little on southern literature for its provender, was solidly established. By the same year, 1946, when Tate went to New York, he and Lytle had reforged the *Sewanee Review* into a distinguished literary and critical review. Ransom with the *Kenyon* was providing the most important critical forum of the 1940s and 50s. By 1948, when the Kenyon School of English had its first session, criticism in the academy, especially the New Criticism, was entrenched. Ransom, as always, was genially democratic. Not only did he invite Eliot to participate in the School of English but F. O. Matthiessen, Lionel Trilling, Richard Chase, and others of differing critical persuasions; and he also recruited the fiercest antagonist of both himself and Tate—Yvor Winters. The year 1948 saw the publication of Tate's *Selected Essays* and of a new collection of critical essays, *The Hovering Fly*. The previous year *The Well Wrought Urn* was published, and at the same time, 1947–1948, Ransom was publishing three of his best essays—"Poetry: The Formal Analysis," "Poetry: The Final Cause," and "The Literary Criticism of Aristotle."

We can safely say that criticism was fixed in the academy by 1948—but more securely in New England and the Middle West than in the South. Only twenty years had passed since Edmund Wilson wrote in the *New Republic*: "What we lack . . . in the United States, is not writers or even literary parties, but simply serious literary criticism. . . . It is astonishing to observe, in America, in spite of our floods of literary journalism, to what extent literary atmosphere is a non-conductor of criticism." Wilson himself remained outside the academy, usually ignoring it; but occasionally he vented his spleen on the academy, as in his famous attack on the Modern Language Association.

Let it not be said that I am suggesting that the triumph of the New Criticism was complete. We all know that even at the height of its influence the New Critics not only battled with the Chicago Aristotelians, the *Partisan Review* critics, and various mythographers such as Northrop Frye but argued among themselves. A classic instance of the differences of opinion among the New Critics is Ransom's essay on Brooks—"Why Critics Don't Go Mad." But we remember that one of the strengths of both the Fugitive and Agrarian groups is the willingness of the principals to be honest with one another in criticism not only of poetry and fiction but of criticism itself.

What happened in the history of the New Criticism's steady successes in its campaigns against the old-style philologists and the historical scholars of other kinds who were the establishment is that the adherents of criticism became part of the establishment. (This also applies to New York critics like Philip Rahv, Alfred Kazin, and Irving Howe.) That was especially true at Yale, where the English faculty was content not to grant Arthur Mizener tenure in 1940 for writing mere criticism but did offer Brooks and Warren posts after the war. Since the war, critics and scholars have gotten along all too well in the university, and they have even brought the writer into the institutional structure, making him a resident—that is, a member of the faculty. The results have not been wholly positive or felicitous by any means, and over the past several decades we have witnessed the institutionalization of literature. The most obvious and ominous result is that literature has been all but strangled under the numbing weight of academic bureaucracy and the academic mind. Thus we have dozens of fictions not only about the writer at work but about the teacher and writer plying their trades within the academy. Most of these narratives, whether solemn or satirical, are vintage fluff. We also have the most self-conscious literature, especially poetry, that has ever been written. The writer these days does not look into his soul but into his navel, the window to his ego; and there he sees the sad history of his protracted adolescence. What we have now is more poems, fictions, critical studies—books of all kinds—and more grants, fellowships, stipends, reduced teaching loads, sabbatical leaves . . . but less literature. Which is to say less literature that is worthy of our attention as readers and students and critics and scholars. The southern New Critics are by no means responsible for this state of affairs. It was their followers—some of them—who turned the New Criticism into an academic exercise. That the New Criticism is regularly under attack these days is part and parcel of the present literary situation. We might briefly define that state by saying that writers are writing chiefly for themselves and for the classroom.

The story that I have told has an obvious point: the achievement of the New Criticism in bringing modern literature and modern criticism into the academy has had unpredictable effects. Courses in contemporary literature and in writing have threatened to overwhelm the curriculum in the typical English department, and criticism has been an activity which often has little or nothing to do with literature. The very success of certain aspects of the New Criticism has produced forces which have led to its rejection in many quarters.

Success is often unpalatable to those who do not share it. But what has offended opponents of the New Criticism far more is the politics and religion of the New Critics. We return to Grant Webster, who calls these men Tory formalists. We hear critics from the left: Bruce Franklin deems the New Criticism "a crude and frankly reactionary formalism"; Louis Kampf, in a triumph of fevered confusion, says that the New Criticism is a tool of an "educational bureaucracy fathered by advanced industrial capitalism," precisely what the Agrarians attacked in the 1930s. Earlier attacks had similar political origins, especially when the southern Agrarians and New Critics were called fascists by their opponents. The most representative incident or series of incidents resulted from the award of the Bollingen Prize to Ezra Pound in 1950. The furor surrounding this event rapidly turned into an attack on modern poetry and the New Criticism. At this time the New Criticism became a convenient bogeyman and whipping boy, not to mention straw man; and it has occupied this unenviable position ever since. I should emphasize that the opponents of the New Criticism have seldom bothered to read anything but *Understanding Poetry*, *The Well Wrought Urn*, and a few anthologized essays. When Ransom or Brooks's critical position is described, for instance, it is presented as being the position that the critic in question held in the 1940s. Now the New Criticism is reduced to a pedagogical tactic when it is not viewed as the product of a conservative conspiracy.

With the southern New Critics we not only realized literature in its fullest possibilities—that it embodies a "reality principle" or a dangerous knowledge of "the dense, actual world," as Ransom put it—but we also saw the possibilities of civilization as opposed to a shabby mass culture.

What the New Criticism chiefly accomplished was to fix the reader's attention on the text. Unfortunately this led to some dreary publications on the part of textual scholars who sometimes seem more interested in the habits of compositors and in end-of-line hyphenation than in what a given author actually wrote and who are unwilling to recognize that any printed text is a collaborative effort to some extent and that no such text is pure. This scientism in its most extreme forms has no more to recommend it than does old-style historical scholarship. The other extreme of the response to the New Critics' insistence that the reader focus his attention on the text first and only later consider the author and the society for which he wrote has of course irrupted of late in the theories of the structuralist and post-structuralist critics. The reader has now become a coauthor, and the text is anything that he wishes to make of it. This form of criticism is not far removed from the old-style impressionism that was practiced by journalists and amateurs early in the twentieth century. The text simply offers the occasion for the critic to explore the limits of his own ego and not so much to describe and judge the literary object that is his alleged subject as to use it for a launching pad. The emphasis is on the critic's generating his own ideas; rather than finding the world's body in poetry, the critic now uses poetry to re-create the world in his own image. The result is that literature is displaced and that criticism, which is properly an attempt to understand and judge the work of art, let us say the poem, becomes more important than literature or at least coequal with it. In "Criticism, Inc." Ransom says that "the critic should regard the poem as nothing short of a desperate ontological or metaphysical manoeuvre." These days criticism has become a desperate ontological and metaphysical manoeuvre, and the structuralists and poststructuralists expect us to admire their preening and pirouetting and to forget that the object of literary criticism is properly literature.

We now have new-style historical scholarship and new-style impressionism. The one is Germanic and scientistic; the other is antihistorical and impressionistic. In both literature gets short shrift, and the informed general reader is forgotten. In the meantime the writer himself, who is now often coddled by foundations and universities alike, is not writing so well as we might expect. The art looks suspiciously like what Davidson predicts in "A Mirror for Artists" when he suggests that with permanent prosperity "we shall have art. We shall buy it, hire it, can it, or . . . manufacture it." This is postmodernism with a vengeance.

In the arid world of the academy one is regularly confronted with new-style critics and writers who view themselves as heroes. In a semiliterate society writing of any kind has become an epic feat, whether or not it is grammatical and whether or not anyone but the author himself can understand it. In such a world it is little wonder that criticism written in turgid and murky periods is taken as the height of profundity, that rambling flatfooted prose broken up on the page to masquerade as poetry is taken as poetry, and that crass and contemptible public behavior by writers is considered commonplace and acceptable.

In such a world the New Critics would seem to have little place. The gentleman is a vanishing species who is as embattled as Ford's last Tories; it may be that there is no place for him in the academy. Now that literature has been institutionalized it may also be that there is no place in the academy for the man of letters. The academy is increasingly a place of specialization, and in such circumstances the man who is at once a writer, a critic, and a lover of literature may tend to be shunted aside. It may be time for him to get out of the academy.

John Crowe Ransom might have said that there is no natural law that forces an artist into the academy or that forces art under the protection of the academy or the foundation. John Gross puts the case for literature very well when he observes that "in a world of increasingly huge centralized institutions, . . . the literary tradition quite simply needs the protection of the universities." "But," he adds, "it would be a sad day if the literary tradition ever came to be positively identified with them." That day is closer than it was when Gross's *The Rise and Fall of the Man of Letters* was published in 1969.

Between 1920 and 1960 the southern New Critics brought modern literature into the academy and at the same time forged a criticism that could interpret and judge that literature. Since then not only modern literature but American literature has been accepted as part of the curriculum, and these salutary developments have been followed by a series of less felicitous changes. Now the typical English department is in the thrall of contemporary literature, and the fragmentation of literature is nearly complete.

At the Fugitive reunion in 1956 Warren observed that the proper function of poetry is to be a fifth column, a fifth column which ultimately contributes to "a moral progress, or a civilizing progress." He went on to remark: "Universities should be fifth columns, but usually aren't." There is occasionally a fifth column within the university—a group like the Fugitives, who constituted what Warren elsewhere calls a university outside the university. It appears time for such fifth columns to establish universities outside the academic bureaucracy and to free literature from the writing programs, the absurdly narrow and specialized courses, the academic critics who are contemptuous of literature, and from institutional bondage in general.

Ransom said at the Fugitive reunion: "We've got now the most exquisite problems that rest on any country that's at peace. . . . And I could wish that we had great literary men engaging in it. . . . It might be the difference between making a civilization and just going along with a shabby culture. . . . I wish we could now start all over." As I have said elsewhere, the Fugitives and Agrarians' greatest contribution lay in giving the South back to the South and making it the greatest country of the American imagination in this century. I believe that writers of their integrity and commitment are needed more than ever in and out of the South—not to engage in public affairs as did Yeats or as did the Agrarians, but to sustain and to elevate the profession of letters and bring to it a necessary style and definition. More important than the profession of letters is literature itself, which is too important to leave in the hands of the foundations and the academy.

A few hardy souls might do it. A few men and women

who are devoted to letters as a vocation and who are indifferent to careerism; a few widely read people who know classical and modern languages and who have enough in common to form a community and yet who are sure enough of themselves not to engage in the usual pursuits of literary backscratching and log-rolling and incest; a few people who are not only dedicated to literature but concerned with social issues; a few writers who understand how the literary marketplace works and how it differs from the academic marketplace. They would be armed not only with knowledge and intelligence but with custom and ceremony. They would also have the example of the southern New Critics and the burden of their accomplishment. In time they might gain a foothold in the present-day academic establishment, putting pedantry, obscurantism, specialization, stodginess, egotism, and other academic habits into disrepute. But the reform of the academy, which would entail making it a place hospitable to the life of the mind, would not be their real purpose. Their aim would be to free literature from the university and let it return to the realm of the imagination—which means to the Republic of Letters and to the reading public as well as to the country of the blue.

There is a constant need for men of letters who can mediate between the academy, the reading public, and the literary estate; men who can practice criticism with enough ease and authority that one can suspend his disbelief in the artifice and artificiality of art and in the subordinate critical enterprise that art—especially literature—necessitates. The job is perpetual, and the augean stable needs to be cleaned out at least once each generation. That is our present plight. In such circumstances we might well wish that the Agrarians were starting over.

Louis D. Rubin, Jr.

I'll Take My Stand: The Literary Tradition

I find myself in somewhat the predicament of the late General Nathan Bedford Forrest, who received for a third time the request of one of his officers for a leave of absence. To which the general responded with the scrawled endorsement, "I told you twicet alredy godamit No." Having written about the Agrarians repeatedly over the course of twenty-five years, including two different introductions to *I'll Take My Stand* as well as a full-length book, I don't know what I shall have to say that I haven't already said before and probably better.

The topic that was assigned to me was "the literary backgrounds of *I'll Take My Stand*." Certainly it does have a considerable literary background, not only in other literature but in the writings of the participants themselves. Upon reflection, however, I believe a better title would be "the literary foreground"—for it seems tolerably clear, now that fifty years have gone by, that the importance of *I'll Take My Stand* is principally as a *literary* work. It is an imaginative work on culture and society, and its survival past its immediate occasion is due, I think, largely to its literary quality. That is, its argument is effective because it makes an imaginative, emotional appeal as well as a logical one, through its use of a controlling image.

Sir Philip Sidney, in "An Apologie for Poetry" (1583), seeking to justify poetry in the face of puritanism and the nascent prestige of science, advanced the thesis that the poet is superior to both the historian and the philosopher, in that "hee coupleth the generall notion with the particuler example. A perfect picture I say, for hee yeeldeth to the powers of the mind, an image of that whereof the Philosopher bestoweth but a woordish distinction: which dooth neyther strike, pierce, nor possesse the sight of the soule, so much as that other dooth." Similarly, what has made *I'll Take My Stand* endure, when other writings making much the same argument have long since receded into the domain of historical documentation, does not lie so much in the political cogency of the social appropriateness of the Agrarian program alone, as in the clarity and passion with which it was set forth. And just as in a good poem, the clarity and passion were not just rhetorical strategies added to sweeten and embellish the idea under discussion, but were integral to the formulation of the idea itself. As in other works of literature, the metaphorical possibility helped to shape the form: that metaphor was predicated upon the symbol of the rural South.

But it was *not* a symbol, someone might object (Donald Davidson once so objected to me). The Agrarians *meant* it literally. They were concerned with a particular time and place, and made specific suggestions and criticisms about that time and place. And I know that at least some of the Agrarians, in sober truth, intended just that. Well, but it was a symbol even so, and its survival is due to the fact that it was. Obviously it cannot have been the practical, topical recommendations of the Agrarian program that have made possible the continuing life of *I'll Take My Stand*. For a polemically designed book to speak to an audience a half century after its occasion, when the agricultural dispensation that the book advocated was not only obsolescent at the time but has now been utterly transformed, it must possess an appeal, must make a commentary on something, that is at once more general and more timeless in its relevance.

The ultimate assertion of *I'll Take My Stand* is in the form of pastoral. It is, fundamentally, a species of pastoral rebuke. Like all pastoral, it was written for and by, not shepherds and swains, even of the dirt-farming variety, but a sophisticated audience of citizens who, like the Agrarians themselves, were dwellers in cities.

We know, of course, that the extent and degree to which the individual Agrarians actively believed in the practicability of a society of farmers differed from participant to participant, and that what they had in mind by "Agrarianism" varied considerably. Stark Young's and Andrew Lytle's notions of what would constitute a traditional rural community were about as far removed from each other as John Ransom's and H. C. Nixon's conceptions of what farmers thought and did and wanted. And so on. We know that the various participants arrived at Agrarianism by different routes, that involvement in the symposium served different needs and played different roles in their careers, and that within a very few years after they jointly took their stand they were headed off in different and sometimes contradictory directions. All this is a matter of record; in retrospect it is in no wise either remarkable or even regrettable.

What brought and held them together, then, was something in the Agrarian scheme that appealed to and, for a time at least, filled certain needs for all of them. It involved rural life, and this not only (perhaps not even principally) for its own sake, but for what it symbolized. It involved the South. It involved a cultural and literary attitude toward nature, and toward cities, of many centuries' standing. And it involved these things *symbolically*, by which I mean that whatever Agrarianism was topically, it stood for something else, and not allegorically but as tangible and real in its own right. As Coleridge says of the symbol, "it always partakes of the reality which it renders intelligible; and while it enunciates the whole, abides itself as a living part of that unity of which it is the representative."

It should not be forgotten that the moving spirits among the twelve Agrarians were principally the literary men— Ransom, Davidson, Tate, Lytle, to a somewhat lesser extent Wade. (Warren's involvement was peripheral; he was in England when the plans were being made.) The others were brought into the venture. Critics of *I'll Take My Stand* dismissed it as merely an affair of poets, which indeed it was. But in actuality this was the source of its greatest strength. For if the poem is, as Tate later defined it, "a formed realm of our experience, the distinction of which is its complete knowledge, the full body of the experience that it offers us," then this attitude can be said to have carried over into the Agrarian undertaking, so that, to an extent at least, the book that resulted made its appeal not only through reasoned expository argument but by embodiment of that argument in an image that could not be dismissed merely as having to do with a farming economy. T. S. Eliot would have it that it is not enough for the poet to look into his heart and write: "One must look into the cerebral cortex, the nervous system, and the digestive tracts." Without insisting that *I'll Take My Stand* is a poem (it is not), I would contend that its conception is significantly *poetic*, as might be expected of a work planned and developed by poets.

Let me look briefly at the literary tradition out of which it came. William Wordsworth, in the Preface to the Second Edition of the *Lyrical Ballads* (1802), made a case for the poetic imagination as being of especial importance in his day. "For a multitude of causes," he declared, "unknown to former times, are now acting with a combined force to blunt the discriminating powers of the mind, and unfitting it for all voluntary exertion, to reduce it to a state of almost savage torpor. The most effective of these causes are the great national events which are daily taking place [*i.e.*, the French Revolution, the Napoleonic Wars], and the increasing accumulation of men in cities, where the uniformity of their occupations produces a craving for extraordinary incident, which the rapid communication of intelligence hourly gratifies." His response as poet was to write poems having to do with nature, the countryside. It was his answer to the Industrial Revolution, and to the increasing specialization of work and narrowing of sensibility involved in modern life as a result of the exploitation of the natural world through applied science.

Now in part that response involved nostalgia, but it was considerably more than that. He set out to write a poetry that "rejoices in the presence of truth as our visible friend and hourly companion. Poetry is the breath and finer spirit of all knowledge; it is the impassioned expression which is in the countenance of all Science. Emphatically may it be said of the Poet, as Shakespeare hath said of man, 'that he looks before and after.' He is the rock of defense for human nature, carrying everywhere with him relationship and love." In short, poetry is to deal with the whole man, not the fragmented personality of the specialist, and the proper locus for that is not in cities but in the countryside, where the fragmentation and dissociation of sensibility have not yet done their work.

Wordsworth was by no means the first English poet to hold up man in nature as spiritual corrective to man in the city. It is a concomitant of English poetry from Shakespeare's time onward; it finds vivid expression in Marvell's "The Garden":

> Meanwhile the mind, from pleasure less,
> Withdraws into its happiness:
> The mind, that ocean where each kind
> Does straight its own resemblance find;
> Yet it creates, transcending these,
> Far other worlds, and other seas;
> Annihilating all that's made
> To a green thought in a green shade.

The transcendental implications of the last two couplets in that stanza, written as they were before the impact of Lockean sensationalism upon subsequent thought, are, to make a bad pun, indeed mind-boggling. Generally, however, nature and the rural scene are attractive because they are more restful, more tranquil and beautiful; the element of metaphysics is not customarily at issue. It is not until the eighteenth century that urban society begins importantly to be seen as constituting a menace to the natural world. I am sure that most of the Agrarians, growing up in the South as I did, were like myself made to memorize lines from Goldsmith's "The Deserted Village":

> Ill fares the land, to hastening ills a prey,
> Where wealth accumulates and men decay;
> Princes and lords may flourish or may fade;
> A breath can make them as a breath has made:
> But a bold peasantry, their country's pride,
> When once destroyed, can never be supplied.

The poem is a response to the Enclosure Laws and the movement of the rural population into the factories of the city. By the close of the eighteenth century the problem of man in nature had assumed proportions so acute that it could no longer be dealt with, as it was in previous times, merely as a mode of sensibility. It became part of the very apprehension of experience itself, forcing a revolution in language, so that poetry, instead of being a commentary upon received aspects of general human experience, must now endeavor to reconstitute that experience in order to give it a totality of meaning unavailable in other, partial forms of apprehension. And that poetry turned increasingly to nature, to the rural experience, not because it was typical of everyday human life, but because in subject matter and terms of reference it offered an *alternative* to what was fast becoming typical and habitual. Instead of nature being used as a term that included human experience—human nature—it now becomes what is *outside* human consciousness. Nature—physical nature—and the mind are separate entities. The poet turns to nature because, not being man-made, it is *real*. Thus Coleridge, in "Frost at Midnight," addresses his child as follows:

> For I was reared
> In the great city, pent 'mid cloisters dim,
> And saw naught lovely but the sky and stars.
> But *thou*, my babe! shalt wander like a breeze
> By lakes and sandy shores, beneath the crags
> Of ancient mountains, and beneath the clouds,
> Which image in their bulk both lakes and shores
> And mountain crags: so shalt thou see and hear
> The lovely shapes and sounds intelligible
> Of that eternal language, which thy God
> Utters, who from eternity doth teach
> Himself in all, and all things in himself.

Needless to say, this newer and more desperate relationship to nature and rurality became part of the American literary experience, for once the frontier had been pushed back to the mountains and the Navigation Acts repealed by the winning of independence, the new nation promptly underwent a rapid recapitulation of the Industrial Revolution, over the course of a few decades rather than across several centuries. Emerson's American Scholar Address is commonly taken as the overt declaration of American literary independence from Europe. Yet what is asserted is precisely the opposition to the fragmentation and specialization of industrial society that so exercised the British poets: "Man is not a farmer, or a professor, or an engineer, but he is all. Man is priest, and scholar, and statesman, and producer, and soldier. In the *divided* or social state these functions are parcelled out to individuals, each of whom aims to do his stint of the joint work, whilst each other performs his. The fable implies that the individual, to possess himself, must sometimes return from his own labor to embrace all the other laborers. But, unfortunately, this original unit, this fountain of power, has been so distributed to multitudes, has been so minutely subdivided and peddled out, that it is spilled into drops, and cannot be gathered. The state of society is one in which the members have suffered amputation from the trunk, and strut about like so many walking monsters,—a good finger, a neck, a stomach, an elbow, but never a man." And to remedy this state of affairs the first recourse that Emerson offers to his scholar is nature. For the rural world can teach him not fragmentation but organic wholeness: "He shall see that nature is the opposite of the soul, answering to it part for part. One is seal and one is print. Its beauty is the beauty of his own mind. Its laws are the laws of his own mind. Nature then becomes to him the measure of his attainments."

For Emerson's friend Thoreau the condition of man under modern commercial society is considerably more desperate. "Men think it essential that the *Nation* have commerce, and export Ice, and talk through a telegraph, and ride thirty miles an hour, without a doubt, whether *they* do or not; but whether we would live like baboons or like men, is a little uncertain. If we do not get out sleepers [*i.e.*, crossties], and forge rails, and devote days and nights to the work, but go to tinkering upon our *lives* to improve *them*, who will build railroads? And if railroads are not built, how shall we get to heaven in season? But if we stay at home and mind our business, who will want railroads? We do not ride on the railroad; it rides on us." Which is Thoreau's industrialized version of "Things are in the saddle, and ride mankind."

I am aware that it is considered an act of semi-treason to suggest the existence of important affinities between the Nashville Fugitives and Agrarians and the New England Transcendentalists, and I am quite aware of the considerable differences between what the New Englanders and the southerners thought concerning what "nature" was, and what man's relationship to it ought to be. There is, for one thing, in the southerners no transcendental escape from the ultimate duality of matter and spirit. Yet it seems undeniable that implicit in the dynamics of the so-called American Renaissance of the mid–nineteenth century was much the same desire to assert the primacy of religious humanism in the face of the mechanistic positivism of applied science, as is exemplified in assertions like the following, from the Statement of Principles to *I'll Take My Stand*:

> Religion is our submission to the general intention of a nature that is fairly inscrutable; it is the sense of our role as creatures within it. But nature industrialized, transformed into cities and artificial habitations, manufactured into commodities, is no longer nature but a highly simplified picture of nature. We receive the illusion of having power over nature, and lose the sense of nature as something mysterious and contingent. The God of nature under these conditions is merely an ami-

able expression, a superfluity, and the philosophical understanding ordinarily carried in the religious experience is not there for us to have.

There were available to the Agrarians, then, powerful literary precedents for thinking and writing about rural society and the natural world as a moral and social corrective to modern urban complexity, for identifying the countryside and life on the land as offering a wholeness of personality and a less mechanistic attitude toward human identity than did urban experience, and for the use of nature as pastoral rebuke to the dehumanizing forces present in mass industrial society. The attitude was part of their thinking, as literary men; the literary tradition to which as young twentieth-century American writers they were heirs embodied that perspective as a mode of language and form.

They were not only young American poets, however; they were *southerners*. The patterns of their community experience had until recently been almost totally rural. From colonial times onward the South had been agricultural; it had remained so when the North had turned to industry. Its leading philosopher had proclaimed the virtuous husbandman as the new republic's social ideal. "Those who labor in the earth," Thomas Jefferson declared, "are the chosen people of God, if ever he had a chosen people, whose breasts he has made his peculiar deposit for substantial and genuine virtue." As for urbanization, "the mobs of great cities add just so much to the support of pure government, as sores do to the strength of the human body." For more than a century after Jefferson the politics of the South was focused upon enunciating the needs of an agricultural community in opposition to the rival claims of an industrial and commercial economy. The response of the South to the Industrial Revolution had not been the factory, but the plantation system. The planter, not the capitalist, had been the Old South's dominant image. And after the defeat of the Civil War, though the notion of a New South of commerce and industry gained powerful adherents, the region had remained largely rural in economy and social attitude. The loss of the war had the effect of retarding any significant industrial development that might otherwise have occurred in accordance with the dynamics of nineteenth-century society; there was no capital available to build the factories.

It was well into the twentieth century before any sizable proportion of the South's population began to derive its income from industrial growth. Thus the life of cities had come very late to the region, and its hold on the southern mind was still of recent vintage, while the suddenness of its impact—the years after the first world war were when it first got really into high gear—dramatized the contrast between rural past and urban present. The old ways, however threadbare, still maintained a powerful hold on the imagination; rural life, in a time of change and confusion, still seemed, in several senses, "natural," a farming economy normal, real. It was the life of big cities that represented the new, the unfamiliar. Thus social experience and literary tradition alike offered, to a group of young men disturbed about their section's future and dismayed at the rampant materialism and commercial opportunism of the 1920s, the Agrarian metaphor. It has been pointed out, and rightly, that the revolt against machine-dominated society and mass dehumanization was very much in the air during the 1920s. The poets that the Fugitives read were full of it, whether in Eliot's "unreal city" in which

> Under the brown fog of a winter dawn,
> A crowd flowed over London Bridge, so many,
> I had not thought death had undone so many . . .

or Pound's "Mauberly" for whom

> All things are a flowing,
> Sage Heraclitus says;
> But a tawdry cheapness
> Shall outlast our days.

or Yeats:

> Locke sank into a swoon;
> The Garden died;
> God took the spinning-jenny
> Out of his side.

The intellectual community of the 1920s was repeatedly being reminded, polemically and diagnostically, that all was not well in the industrialized and progressive Western World. The message was implicit in Lawrence's novels, in *The Great Gatsby*, *Manhattan Transfer*, "The Great God Brown," *The Sun Also Rises*, "The Second Coming," "The Waste Land"; it was explicit in the disquisitions of Lewis Mumford, Walter Lippmann, Joseph Wood Krutch, Hilaire Belloc, James Truslow Adams, Ralph Borsodi, Dean Inge, Stuart Chase. There can be no question but that the Agrarian venture was part and parcel of the overall protest of thoughtful people against the unchecked disintegrative forces in Western industrial life, forces that would eventuate in the Great Depression that struck just as the Agrarian symposium was coming to fruition.

What the Agrarians had as their own, however, was the tangible experience of the southern community as it confronted, belatedly and fiercely, the impact of modernity. Thus they possessed an image, a focus for their own critique, which not only grounded their response in the actualities of American historical experience but in so doing protected them from the abstract panaceas of Marxism and Fascism that proved so catastrophic to much of the social thinking of the 1930s. If there was an element of abstraction in Agrarianism, as in all ideologies, it was largely held in check by the palpable and tangible social experience of the southern community involvement that all the Agrarians inherited by birth and upbringing. Agrarianism may have been a concept; the southern community, with its rural ties and historical loyalties, was substantial, a thing of flesh and blood. And if, as young intellectuals of the 1920s, the Agrarians had experienced something of the sense of rootlessness and dissociation that Malcolm Cowley has described as an "exile . . . from any society to which they could honestly contribute and from which they could draw the strength that lies in shared convictions," their response was to assert an identity with a community that for them was not so irretrievably lost that it possessed no meaning except nostalgia. They were moderns, but they were southerners; they could still think of themselves as having a place to go to.

Whatever the literal practicality of Agrarianism might have been at the close of the third decade of the twentieth century, there can be little doubt that it represented, for the twelve southerners who took part in the 1930 symposium, considerably more and other than an intellectual formulation, a strategic device for developing an argument. It was a *cause*, demanding, and receiving, of its adherents emotional engagement as well as rational assent. In the long run the decision to use the Agrarian identification may have blunted the force of the participants' critique of industrial dehumanization through exposing it to ridicule because of the anachronistic economics. For it was as a rebuke to the uncritical espousal of material Progress that *I'll Take My Stand* had something important to say to its readers, and not as a social and economic program. We know that Tate and Warren made a last-minute attempt to have the title of the symposium changed so as to avoid the overt southern identification that came from the echoing of the war song of the Confederacy. The use of that title, Tate warned, would enable hostile critics "only to draw portraits of us plowing or cleaning a spring to make hash of us before we get a hearing." And of course he was right; that, so far as the immediate reception of the book is concerned, is exactly what happened.

The argument, however, leaves out the obvious truth that it was precisely the southern identification, neo-Confederate associations and all, that accounts for much of the book's cohesion and passion, for it enabled the participants to draw what for *all* of them was a powerfully felt community identification. What the details of the "South" meant for each of them differed from participant to participant, but for all of them it involved vigorous emotional as well as intellectual loyalties, grounded in a common geography, drawing upon a shared sense of social identity, and given form and feeling by a passionately shared historical mythos.

John Shelton Reed, in his excellent paper, has described this element as something closely resembling nationalism, which he properly characterizes as one of the central forces of the past several hundred years. I am not so certain that nationalism is precisely the term for what he is describing, however; certainly the Confederate loyalty was present, more so for some than for others, but I do not believe that the Agrarians considered themselves as any other or less than Americans *in* their southern loyalties. Sectionalism, however much it was considered a "bad" word (the "good" word was regionalism), comes perhaps closer than nationalism: the community identification, independent of the political concomitants usually associated with the term nationalism, is what was uppermost. I can't really see the

Agrarians as the equivalent of young Scottish nationalists plotting to steal the Stone of Scone. (Indeed, there have been historians who have declared that even the wartime Confederates were not really nationalists at heart, and that the defeat of the Confederacy was due in important respects to the absence of a true sense of nationalism on the part of the people of the South; the Confederacy has been described as having come into being and subsequently disintegrated because of states' rights.)

The important point, however, which I believe Mr. Reed is getting at, is that anyone who attempts to strip *I'll Take My Stand* of its distinctively southern character, and fails to recognize that the Agrarian identification was a powerful and probably essential symbolic element in the involvement of the participants in the common enterprise, ignores a great deal of what has kept this book alive for a half-century. The agrarian community provided an image for what the participants cherished about the South, and the South in turn constituted a symbol for qualities that were lacking in mass technological society, and that were very much menaced by the forces of urban industrialism. Stark Young's caveat—"we defend certain qualities not because they belong to the South, but because the South belongs to them"—is only half true. In the minds of most of the young Agrarians no such distinction could be made.

As for just what those qualities are, Tate has used the term "religious humanism," which is appropriate, I think, but needs to be supplemented by the word *southern*. There have been many attempts to characterize the cultural and social ideals of religious humanism in relationship to the South. Tate himself has referred to "knowledge carried to the heart," and has summarized them in his description of what Aeneas takes with him after the destruction of Troy:

> —a mind imperishable
> If time is, a love of past things tenuous
> As the hesitation of receding love.

Earlier, Henry Timrod offered the following formulation:

> . . . the type
> Whereby we shall be known in every land
> Is that vast gulf which lips our Southern strand,
> And through the cold, untempered ocean pours
> Its genial streams, that far off Arctic shores
> May sometimes catch upon the softened breeze
> Strange tropic warmth and hints of summer seas.

I like best John Ransom's way of putting it:

> True, it is said of our Lady, she ageth.
> But see, if you peep shrewdly, she hath not stooped;
> Take no thought of her servitors that have drooped,
> For we are nothing; and if one talk of death—
> Why, the ribs of the earth subsist frail as a breath
> If but God wearieth.

In Ransom's uniting of poetry, religion, ritual, the land and southern history in a single developed image, we have, I think, not only the themes of *I'll Take My Stand*, but the underlying values that Agrarianism symbolized. In identifying the Agrarian symposium as a form of pastoral, shaped to remind a modern community of the dangers of dehumanization, I mean to insist that *I'll Take My Stand* is, finally, a poetic work. Wordsworth described poetry as "a homage paid to the native and naked dignity of man, to the grand elementary principle of pleasure, by which he knows, and feels, and loves, and moves." (By pleasure Wordsworth meant not mere sensory enjoyment but the passion and knowledge of the mind of man in nature.) Not all the Agrarians were poets; not all were literary men. But what the terms of the enterprise drew from all of them was the fusion of knowledge and feeling that characterizes the poetic imagination. The cogency of the argument cannot be separated from the disciplined passion with which it is articulated. That is why, fifty years after it was set forth, we continue to read the book.

Lyle Lanier   Andrew Lytle   Robert Penn Warren
Cleanth Brooks, Moderator

DISCUSSION   The Agrarian-Industrial
Metaphor: Culture, Economics, and
Society in a Technological Age

Mr. Brooks: I think I met the three gentlemen here with me
all at one time. I was rooming for a short time with a senior
at Vanderbilt in the fall of 1924, Bill Clark, and I believe that,
Andrew, you and Lyle and Red, all were there together.
And how my eyes popped! I learned a lesson from that
which I hope I shall remember today. I looked up, way up,
at the three of you. I was impressed with your dignity and
power. You are still, whether you like it or not, my seniors. I
shall try to keep that fact in mind. So I hope that in our discussion of the issues raised by *I'll Take My Stand* after fifty
years the question will not have to be returned to me too
often.

We do have a lot of options, however. Let me mention
some and then I will try to stop talking for a while.

There is the whole question of ecology, though that is a
term that I believe the Agrarians never used. Nevertheless,
that is what they were talking about. In this matter they
were prophetic. Maybe somebody wants to talk about that.

Several years ago the magazine *Shenandoah* ran a series of
statements by the Agrarians entitled *Twenty Years After:
What Changes Would You Make?* I was amazed at the number
of Agrarians who said we should have dropped back to a
deeper line of defense; we ought to have talked more about

religion. Maybe that issue ought to come up here. And surely, in the brilliant papers that we've been hearing the last couple of days, much has been said about the split within the human psyche—and within the culture—the split between means and ends, facts and values. That situation might be something which would be thoroughly relevant to a present-day interpretation of *I'll Take My Stand*.

At any rate, what I and the audience want to hear, of course, are your second and third thoughts. What remains of value? What things now, if you were rewriting your essays, would you say instead of what you said then?

Mr. Lanier: It occurred to me that it might be interesting to talk a little bit about the background of *I'll Take My Stand*, but I would like to say first that I've been sitting through the last three sessions and listening with increasing wonderment, and a sense of humility, to these remarkably fine papers about this document which was contrived somewhat in a hurry, although there was a lot of discussion. I think we have all been amazed that it has held up over the years, and certainly particularly proud that so many unusual things could have been said about the publication at this late date. We are deeply indebted to the participants on the program, to the organizers, to the university, to the National Endowment for the Humanities for making this occasion possible.

Now, just a brief word about some background. There were national economic and cultural kinds of conditions, of course, in the late 1920s, '28, '29, and of course 1930, that created crises of one sort or another. People were groping for some means to respond—some way to behave—in relation to these unusual conditions. There were local irritants, among which I might list a publication called *The Advancing South*, and associated kinds of activities in which the effort was being made to industrialize the South and to bring into the South some of the evils, as we saw them, of industrialism in the rest of the country. There was a problem of what to do in the way of the adoption of some kind of position, some kind of stance. What do you do in the face of these conditions? There was the choice of Marxism, which had a stock kind of criticism of the industrial system. It was not congenial—I don't need to elaborate on that, some of the papers have referred to it—this was not very congenial to us. There was also the possibility of cultivating a rationalistic kind of analysis, in the mode of the social sciences. People talked about regionalism at the University of North Carolina, some kind of understanding of industrialism and the crisis of civilization that seemed to be emerging at that time—following John Dewey and others—in the belief that gradually an incremental kind of improvement would be made that somehow would just diffuse itself through the population and through the leadership of the country and gradually bring about the elimination of the ills of industrialism.

Neither of these approaches appealed to us. They didn't appeal to me, although I was a kind of fledgling social scientist, a would-be psychologist. There still was the problem that there was nothing in psychology that seemed to me to hold any kind of promise for an effective way of responding to this sort of situation. This, then, was the background of our concerns.

I recall that for two years I lived in New York at the same time that Allen Tate was there, and we talked a great deal and came to a common view about the Marxist approach prevalent among the New York intelligentsia. Out of this emerged, I think, an effort to find a third way, another way. Perhaps it's a fourth way. And I was attracted to the literary group, not being literary, because it seemed to me that they were in the process of formulating what has been described by Louis Rubin, and others, as a metaphor; some way of conceiving a kind of society which would effectively counteract the conditions we were concerned about.

So there was a complex combination of factors, but I think we all came together on the common ground that is expressed in the introductory manifesto. And it was a sort of happening. I don't know that this sort of happening would occur again: a coalescence of circumstances and people and conditions which would bring about the creation of this kind of work.

I want to talk about two points just by way of some supplementation of what I had to say before in *I'll Take My Stand*. I describe my general position now as being: "Still standing, but not standing still," at least, not quite. I think the first point is to ask about the indictment of industrialism which is found in *I'll Take My Stand*—pretty highly generalized, highly effective, in my view, as comments on such ills. These have been enumerated in one way or another in most of the preceding papers, and I won't review them— but how does the inventory of the ills of industrialism found in *I'll Take My Stand* compare with what might be said today? I think it's fair to say that *I'll Take My Stand* is a gross understatement of the conditions we face today. There were developments later that we did not and could not have imagined in applied science, technology, and industrial development. I mention just two, perhaps two of the most powerful sorts of developments in the whole field of technology: one, the computer; the discoveries in solid state physics which brought about computerization and control systems, and this kind of thing. And the other, of course, was nuclear science and engineering, which changed the whole ball game completely. These were without our ken, and I think in a way the combination has created a threat to society, to civilization, which, had we known about it, we certainly would have discussed. But the situation is now far more serious, and obviously, you know from reading the newspapers, far more difficult to control. We have the degradation of the environment, the depletion of nonrenewable resources, which was not so acute a problem in those days, when there seemed to be infinite resources. There is talk in *I'll Take My Stand* about depredations committed upon natural resources, but it was different in kind, and certainly in scale, from what would be said today. The industrial impairment of human health, all the kind of things that you read about, pollution and food additives and the science of chemistry and the sciences related to radiation, all of these hazards were existent, but not extremely prominent at that time. There was not the kind of urgency about them that we have now. Urbanization and all of the ills of urban society related to industrialism were acute problems, talked about a lot, but we did not then have in so extreme a form the urban ghetto, the ghetto society, which is a combination of a welfare society and a crime society, throwing in drugs and a few others things that get involved. Here we have apparently a national acceptance of this kind of situation, with the problem being somehow to maintain those who live there with better housing, sufficient food, some kind of subsistence. But few ask, What about changing this whole situation? I'm sure we would have been more explicit in trying to articulate what might be done to change those conditions. A lot is being said about it now, but for the most part it seems to me that the programs are merely ameliorative.

I mentioned nuclear science, the nuclear age, which has come upon us, and which threatens, of course, the whole planet. I don't need to elaborate on that. Robert Heilbroner

has talked about this, I think very well, in his little book—
An Inquiry into the Human Prospect: the fact that at the rate at
which resources are now being utilized, and energy generated, the increase in the temperature eventually—given the
growth in population and the kind of industrial expansion
that we hear talked about—will create intolerable conditions. There will be so much heat that life on the planet will
become impossible.

So there is not merely the threat to values and to the
kinds of society we would like to live in, there is the threat
to the planet, to all civilization, and a lot would be said
about that kind of thing. And I could go on. I have assembled a whole litany of things here, but I won't take the
time now to recite it.

Mr. Brooks: You would say, then, Lyle, that as a matter of
fact the great recent developments in science and technology that have occurred since 1930, haven't made *I'll Take
My Stand* obsolete, but have actually sharpened the issues
which were raised in that book.

Would you like to talk to that, Red?

Mr. Warren: I won't add much to it, but I would certainly
say that in my opinion it's totally true. I think we were very
weak on the side of suggestions, on the positive side, what
to do about things; I think we were dead center on the
negative side, as it was focused on the implicit dangers, the
growing dangers of the kind of society we were creating. I'll
come back to that at a different angle in a little while when I
get a chance to, but I agree totally. I think it's very important
to know the negative—the provocations of the book and
the positive suggestions of the book.

And then a third question: the regional relation of the
book to this particular region and to the late Confederate
States; that's another question, which I think is a peripheral

and accidental question, [but was] as far as the book was concerned, in its heart, its basic quality.

Mr. Brooks: Andrew.

Mr. Lytle: Well, several years before Allen Tate died, he and I were discussing this matter, and although nobody considered himself a prophet, we seemed far better prophets than we knew.

Now I'd like to sort of add here that we wrote *I'll Take My Stand*, but all of us had other work to do. We were and are not specialists, at all. About seven years after the publication of the book, our engagement with the agrarian cause waned. Everybody scattered, doing his own work, and it took a little while to get back, to find—at least on my part—any further interest in it. Recently I've been thinking about it. My particular interest was in the small farm as the source of the strength of the state. Now you don't have any family-sized farms, you don't have any private businesses, everything initiates from afar. Now you go through the countryside and it's empty. There may be a few people in it, but they have no community. The whole family as a unit of society has been damaged almost unto death. That is a grave situation. The alternative is the servile state or the police state, which we are fast moving into.

Think about any university campus. I remember here at Vanderbilt old Cap Alley, the only campus guard, used to go about in a go-cart and shoot sparrows out of the trees. Now the vice-chancellor might be picked up by the police looking like an errant young boy.

The family is of first importance. It has to have location, has to be fixed somewhere. You can have a family without it, but location strengthens the family because you have gathered about a fixation on a spot of land, or even the inheritance of a business, the history of a family. Now, no family is any older than another, but the family that sees itself as older and has some inheritance that is worth passing on to the generations, is the family that is stable; such families make stable a society. You've got to have that old grandmother in the back room saying, "Have your tongue pulled out before you lie," don't you see?

Mr. Brooks: Andrew, that's a long way from—what do you call it?—permissive education, progressive education? They don't furnish those grandmothers and they wouldn't let them say that, anyway. Red.

Mr. Warren: One small matter in this question. I used to know a man who was, I think, a psychologist by trade originally, but he was employed by the government at the time I knew him. He was an official on a team of psychologists and sociologists, and such, which was investigating the background of the national merit scholarship winners. What made those winners? They came from all parts of the country, all sorts of schools, all sorts of ethnic backgrounds, all sorts of this and that. What was the common denominator that made them scholarship winners? I was having a chat with him once about this and asked him, "What did you find?" He said, "We found only one thing: somebody behind the child." He said it might be an illiterate cook, you see, it might be an illiterate cowhand in Wyoming, it might be an old grandmother who couldn't read and write, or it might be a learned grandfather. You couldn't tell who it was. Somebody who could talk to the child and give that child a long-range sense of himself and the confidence to face a long thing ahead; some person is behind that child, maybe a teacher, as it was in Dreiser's case. Somebody. Some person. If you destroy a whole sense of "person" behind "child" you have destroyed "child"; that was his point. And behind these young geniuses that win national merit scholarships, there is somebody. That doesn't mean education, it means character, it means some sense of self-dependency. "It's up to you son, and don't quit. Stick with it." A sense of giving that child a personality that could take hard knocks and keep its direction. He said, "This is the only thing we can find so far that binds them together." That means a certain kind of concentrated life, family or otherwise, but somebody who has some kind of what stands for a family relationship to the child. I would just mark that as a small piece of evidence.

Mr. Brooks: Very important evidence, it seems to me. Lyle.

Mr. Lanier: I will shift to another topic. I will complete the indictment of industrialism by saying that it seems to me, and seemed to a good many people in the 1970s, that even more critical than the inherent contradictions in our industrialized society which I mentioned a few moments ago is the hypothesis, which is widely debated now, that this society, and all industrial societies, capitalist, communist, what not, are coming towards a stage of no growth. Most of our political leaders agree that there must be growth, endless, progressive growth, which is the fundamental thesis underlying the industrial system. The minute the system stops growing, in the form of increasing productivity per worker, you begin to have distribution problems, you have inequities in who has what, not merely within nations but among nations. I think the evidence is accumulating that the rate of growth is receding. In part this is because the vast rate and level of economic growth that has been achieved in the industrial societies has been achieved at the cost of the social ills that have been enumerated. We have not paid—that is, the industrial system has not paid—for cleaning up the environment. It has not paid for all the damage done to society. Now the chickens are coming home to roost.

Well, simple arithmetic will show you that this increasing

cost of repairing the damage to society is going to help slow down the rate of growth. But are we coming towards a rate of zero growth, no growth? There are good arguments by reputable economists, that that is the case—sound statistical evidence. There are arguments and beliefs on the other side. The conservative think-tank, I think it's called the American Enterprise Institute for Public Policy, will have a whole list of counterarguments that growth is just endless. All you need to do is to free economic enterprise and let people go out and exploit the earth and utilize resources more productively, develop more and better robots. They even have robots developing robots, not just regulating them.

Mr. Warren: Quite literally.

Mr. Lanier: Yes, this is how we are going to overcome the Japanese superiority in production of automobiles: robotizing industry.

Mr. Brooks: Wouldn't it be helpful to have all the consumers turned into consuming robots and so get rid of that nuisance, the human race?

Mr. Lanier: Well, I think I share the opposite point of view. I believe that we are coming into a phase of what has been called, in one definition, postindustrial society. The origination of this term by Daniel Bell, a distinguished sociologist, gave it the opposite meaning to the one that I hold. He envisaged a society in which there would be tremendous increase in the rate of growth of science and technology towards the eventual development of a technical intelligentsia that would be able to exert worldwide control through the use of geniuses of sorts. I guess this is a kind of plagiarism on Plato's philosopher-kings, except that these would be technician kings.

Well, that's one meaning of postindustrial society: super industrialism, except that this would be rationalized; it would be controlled by rational men and rational means, and in this way you would be able to produce a good life, effectively distribute goods, *et cetera*, *et cetera*. Now, the other meaning is that postindustrial society is going to be one in which this aggressive effort to increase growth, to accumulate wealth, is simply a contradiction in terms. It cannot continue, for the reasons that I have cited: the exhaustion of resources, the population situation, all of the by-products of this kind of development will simply lead to mass suicide.

If that is true, as I believe it to be—and there is no way to prove this—we face, I think one of the most serious debates of our time. All of our presidential candidates, except Barry Commoner, have subscribed to the growth hypothesis—that is, they cannot admit that the country is going to stop growing. Well, it isn't going to stop growing, in a sense. Furthermore, there are other kinds of growth than economic growth that do not have the sorts of costs that economic industrial growth has. But if you adopt the assumption that a postindustrial society is conceivable in which human values have to be changed, people have to become more parsimonious; as Heilbroner says, maybe the work ethic has been overdone. There has got to be a revolution in values.

Well, the other side of the wheel we were arguing for in *I'll Take My Stand* is coming around now, it seems to me, towards some neo-agrarian kind of society involving decentralization of the population, and the use of solar energy rather than nuclear energy. And solar energy is, by its nature, dispersed widely. The sun is everywhere.

I could go on with a lot of other illustrations of kinds of needs and even kinds of developments—not very pronounced, but you do read about people who are moving out of the cities. Some of them tend to be cultists and they are ridiculed; but there are serious people who are thinking about getting out of the urban rat race and trying to live a simpler, more rewarding life. And I would maintain, if I had two or three hours, that there's a lot of logic and reason in thinking that there is movement in this direction and that the prediction of *I'll Take My Stand*, the forecast, the idea, is at least thinkable on the positive side as well as on the negative side. It is in the mainstream, if this notion of the postindustrial situation has any validity. I think it does.

Mr. Warren: May I interject something here along that line? A year ago, I guess it was, I read a report in *Time* magazine about a research foundation which periodically conducted surveys to find out if people were happy in cities. The report was important as a piece of news because for the first time in their every four or five year survey of this question, and for the first time in New York City, well over 50 percent, 60-odd percent, said they wanted out. Now, most of the people wouldn't know what "out" is, you know. They wouldn't know what "out" is. They just want out. Out. This applied, apparently, not merely to the penthouse group or the bottom-of-the-slum group. Somehow the experts had balanced these returns so that they applied as a percentage of the whole population, balanced, whatever you do to it to make it sound the way you want. Anyway, it wasn't what you wanted. It was what they wanted. They wanted out.

Now, where do you go? Well, God knows, they didn't know how to go. Like a little colony that came up in the mountains of Vermont and were sowing garden seed in October. That held no future. They finally burned up half the colony in a barn by having a dog—dogs or cats or babies—knock over old rickety orange crates on which were coal oil lamps or candles. A friend of mine, a nice man who knows all about Vermont life, called on them trying to help them out. The dog defecated before his feet. He got up and nobody moved. He got up and got a shovel and old paper and said, "Get it up." And they said, "Oh, don't touch that, that's nature. Don't touch it."

Well, that's one kind of romance of nature, but it's not found to be popular.

Mr. Brooks: In other words, agrarianism is not brainless and mindless, as often thought. If you get a truly brainless and mindless agrarianism you get the situation that Red has just illustrated.

Mr. Warren: They burned it down and five of them died in it. A dog switched his tail. I don't know how it happened.

A topic I want to introduce, for what it amounts to—I wasn't in on the early days of the discussion of *I'll Take My Stand*, I was far off in England and doing something quite different, but they asked me, kindly, would I write a little piece for it? Well, I wrote a little piece that I haven't read since I read proof on it. But the subject of that little piece stuck very closely with the matter of race, and I've written two little books on race since, and I have spent several years working on those books, and interviewing and reading books about the subject. But that's not the point I'm getting at. The point I'm getting at is the question that is implicit in the symposium, the old symposium is: what happens to people? Now, I'm not talking about race. I'm changing that subject to people in general. I'm speaking of a dehumanizing process, a depersonalizing process, that goes on in our society more and more acutely. When Cleanth, R. W. B. Lewis, and I were writing a history of American literature a few years ago, *American Literature: The Makers and the Making*, as we were doing the reading, going on and on and talking about it in weekly and biweekly meetings, certain questions were raised in my mind. Here are a few quotations I'd like to leave with you which raised one question very early.

Take Emerson—now, when I appeal to Emerson, that means I am in desperate straits. Except I did find a paragraph that summed something up for me perfectly in Emerson. And God help me, I had done a great injustice. I thought there was nothing for me in Emerson, but I found this. I will read the quotation to you. It is called "Considerations by the Way" from the book called *The Conduct of Life*. This is the quotation:

> Leave off this hypocritical prating about masses. Masses are rude, lame, unmade, pernicious in their demands and influence. I wish not to concede anything to them, but to tame, drill, divide and break them up . . .

That sounds pretty fascistic, doesn't it? But the next line, next sentence: ". . . and break them up and make individuals out of them."

Now that's what our society has been doing, is *to concede nothing to them*, is *to make them lame, unmade and pernicious in their demands*—and *not individuals*. Individuals—to continue—

> Individuals, I do not wish any masses at all, that's the ideal condition, but honest men only. No shovel-handed, narrow-brained, gin-drinking, million stockingers or mazzeroni, at all. Where is this hurrah for masses as masses? Let us have considered votes of single men, spoken on their honor and their conscience.

This is the old dream. Jefferson would have understood what he was saying.

Now, a little later there came a famous man called Whitman. Let's don't forget the word *mass* in here and *masses*, that's the key word. If Jefferson had read the following passage from this ambiguously sexed mystic, Mr. Whitman, he would have been very puzzled. "I celebrate myself and sing myself. Now, what I assume, you should assume, we are all alike, exactly; and every atom belonging to me belongs as good to you."

But even worse, suppose Jefferson had gotten this far along in reading Whitman; if Jefferson had, he would have been despairing. In the poem called *Long, Too Long America*, Whitman really kicked over the apple cart. "For who, except myself, has yet conceived what your children enmasse really are?"

Well, who had conceived it? Not Jefferson, not the honest man who gives thought to his honest vote by his honest conscience, but what? The children of TV, of lies, of this, of that; the manipulated masses. When you say "mass" you mean what can be manipulated: the advertising man's prey, the public relation man's prey. Such a man wrote *The Selling of the President*. His job was to create a new Nixon. Remember that book? They created Nixon. That wasn't the real Nixon at all; it was the created Nixon. How to sell Nixon? You make him over, you change his personality so he will be suitable for a chunk of masses. Not honest men giving their vote on their honor and their conscience; rather, the masses voting for an image.

Or, think of what Boorstin's book called *The Image* says about America. It's a great comic work. Leaves you in stitches. Every five pages you break out laughing. You just can't be silent for a moment, you have to take time out and recover your wind. But there's that side.

Mr. Brooks: Red, may I throw a little fuel on that fire you have been burning so nicely? I know a very wise man who gave a talk about the common man in which he made a great many of my friends at the university very angry because he was deprecating the common man. So somebody got up and threatened him and said, "Give us an example of this common man." And what did my friend say? "Adolf Hitler"—who was a pretty skillful manipulator of the masses.

Mr. Lytle: There is no such thing as a common man; can't be.

Mr. Warren: That's what Emerson hoped and what Jefferson thought.

Mr. Lytle: You've got the plain man; the "common man" is an abstraction, isn't it?

Mr. Warren: Mass man.

Mr. Lytle: Yes, that's right.

Mr. Warren: Let's just use that word, for my convenience, anyway.

Mr. Lytle: Okay.

Mr. Warren: I have one more reference. I can't quote it, I don't have the quotation, but it's from *Poets of Barbarism* by Santayana. Of course, he's not very kind to some kinds of poets. He thought all poets were going downhill from Athens on, and he thought even less of current-day poetry, including all people I know. But anyway, he said of Whitman: Whitman was preaching a mysticism in which all people are alike, the mass. Whitman belongs to me, belongs to you; we are all alike, and we all have some kind of mystic power together. The housing magazines and the selling of nylon hose. Selling those things. It's all trade, making the new self—the new you. The new you is very significant in this connection. There's no real you, just the new image of you, which you can create by drinking more milk or wearing this brand of pantyhose. Something makes a new you. A man can get a new kind of suit or grow a new head of hair, if possible.

Santayana said that Whitman, in his mysticism of the mass, stands for the new world in which there are no distinctions, where you can't tell a man from a woman. Even that distinction is wiped out. We are moving in that direction, quite clearly, in appearance and otherwise, a world of no distinction. But the sole business of intelligence is to make distinctions. It is to make distinctions, significant distinctions.

There is a good and a bad Whitman. The bad-boy Whitman wanted to wipe out distinction: one union, that flag over us, that one aspect of it and one "horse." He may have been right about that. He clearly was betting on the right horse. But to make no distinction whatsoever, good or bad —all the same—turns us into the prey of the advertising man, the political manipulator: Hitler.

Mark Twain gave us the last picture. We need nothing beyond *A Connecticut Yankee in King Arthur's Court* to see what happened. Twain didn't mean to write that book; the book wrote him. It wound up with the horror of Hank Morgan, the technician, who became boss, with armed janissaries defending him against the "common people" non-mass— including knights and serfs, and God knows what. With this battle of the Sandbelt he stands in the falling mists of the remnant of horse flesh, man flesh, and armor. And later awakening to his own century he remembers only a dream of the happy time he spent by the green woods in Old England, riding by the side of the girl Sandy. That's the only dream left. His main obsession is the human muck. The rest is all "human muck," except that one dream he remembers. Human muck. That's where it winds up, in the battle of the Sandbelt.

Well, when is this thing going to happen? The first man who pushes the button on the bomb will start the battle of the Sandbelt. You've probably had that line of thought, there, I imagine.

Mr. Brooks: One of the things that strikes me about this controversy that surged early around *I'll Take My Stand*, when it appeared—and it keeps up—is this: that what the good life is can be taken for granted. It's terribly important to enlist all our energies in finding the means to promote or secure the good life. And goodness knows, that's important, but it's always taken for granted—almost always taken for granted—that any fool knows what "the good life" is. I think that is the great lie that has been foisted on all of us, that you can leave values and the purposes of life to take care of themselves.

Would you say something to that theme?

Mr. Lytle: Well, I read the Emerson business, about the individual man, which you presented. That's an honest man, separate, but there is nothing to sustain that man. A southerner would know you would have to have property, something to lose so you would be careful how you would vote and protect yourself. I think that would be the great distinction between New England and the South at that time. And that is gone, that is gone.

Mr. Warren: Let's leave something to Emerson—let's leave a few words to him, anyway.

Mr. Lytle: Okay, I leave him to you. Now, here's something I would like to mention. Nobody could really have taken a firm religious position at the time *I'll Take My Stand* was written. It was not in the air and not in our minds. I don't really think that Allen Tate took a position as a religious man, at that time, if I may say so.

Mr. Warren: He didn't refer to it. He referred to religion as what was lacking in the southern picture.

Mr. Lytle: Yes.

Mr. Warren: Historians, I think, would certainly agree that to that extent there was nothing to bind the Confederacy together, in the end, except the abstraction; nothing to bind them together otherwise. And the defeatism of the last year was pretty clear.

Mr. Lytle: Well, yes.

Mr. Warren: Compared to the Irish, for instance, who had the Catholic Church to bind them together.

Mr. Lytle: That's true. I've been thinking a little about this in terms of religion. In the first place, the opposite of love is not hatred, it's power. It's this power that you've been talking about. Now, every office has to have a power to execute it. But this is the power that accumulates and gives you the power of money. For example, the Puritans, that's what I'm coming around to. I think they are Satanists, and I think Satan was the first Puritan.

Let me tell you what he does. Now, mind you, all of our ancestors, Scotch-Irish, and many others in this country, have Puritan blood in them, but they are not absolute. I'm taking an absolute position on this. The trouble is that the Puritan puts evil in the object. He puts it in the deck of cards, or a bottle of whiskey, or bodies moving in the dance, and he puts it in the rose—well, I won't go on and make bad verse on that.

But God made these things and they cannot be bad in themselves. They are either good or bad in the human heart and the human will, where you have the cooperating opposites by means of which we all live.

We've been speaking a little on this occasion of myths which contain basic truths about the human situation. In the Garden of Eden, if you presume that the potentate of the Garden—nobody knows God, nobody's seen him or anything, but let's say he reduced himself to a game, then, and made this Garden and became the potentate in it. And as any artist does, he finds that he has done more than he thinks, perhaps—at least what he has not expected to do.

So he got there and he walked in the cool of the day, but he got lonesome, so he made this man like him—spit on some dirt and made him. But this man found that he had to have something of his own, and God gave him power. God gave him power over the beasts of the field and the birds in the air and the things that swam and the things that crawled. But you know what God did not do? You look at Genesis carefully. God did not give him any power over the flora. God named Adam and Adam named these beasts of the field: that was power. But God didn't give Adam power over the things that grew, which were there before Adam. If He had, Adam would have had power over the two trees at the center of the Garden. Then there would have been no problem, no exile. It would have been all right to eat that apple, don't you see?

Now, to carry this a little further, God—not God, but the potentate—was learning more and more, and he saw this fellow needed some company so he made a woman. And the great mistake he made there was that he should have named the woman. He let Adam name it and produce this continuous kind of—well, lovers' quarrel. The serpent caught on to that; the beautiful fellow with the beautiful head and slimy tail, stuck his head out of the tree. And what did he offer? He offered the object in itself: the apple, appetite, you see. And satiation of appetite is the loss of innocence. When Adam ate that apple, you see, in that was not only appetite, it was a sensibility, by means of which we reach each other in the world. So he put appetite there, and out of that came some of the trouble; that is to say, it was not for turnip greens and corn bread, mind you, it was for power. Adam and Eve were to live as the gods, knowing both good and evil.

Fine. Now, the ultimate—I'm not going to continue this, but the ultimate progression of that is in the industrial factory, the industrial object, which is a good in itself but it takes no account of the man who is forced to serve it.

Mr. Brooks: Andrew, I have heard nearly all my life from

friends of yours about you and Rutherford County meta-physics. And now, with this exposition by the old master himself, of Rutherford County theology, I am stunned. Brilliant performance.

Mr. Lanier: Cleanth, I would like to add a footnote to Red's example about the survey of people who felt, in a sense, powerless, they wanted out. I listened to a radio program on public broadcasting in Washington about a year and a half ago. I happened to be there a month, sort of incarcerated—couldn't escape. And this station conducted a series of interviews, mainly with black people who were leaving Washington, D.C., mostly to go to the South. I wish I had a tape recording of this particular one who, when asked, "Why are you leaving?"—he was a fairly well-to-do person; he had an adequate living, I judge—said, "I want to go home. I want to go to some place where I'm not afraid to go out on the streets at night. Where I live now, a kind of middle-class community, we simply don't dare to go out on the street. We barely know our neighbors next door. We've lived here, and yet it ain't living. I want to go home where my people are, where I'll have some . . ."—I forget his language, but what he meant was: some human association, some security, some kind of sense of being in a place which was meaningful to him. And there was a succession of these interviews in the same vein.

Now, this represents only a trickle, in the national sense, I suppose, but the impulse is definitely there: the cultists, all kinds of people—queer ones—have attempted to exploit it; but there has been no really organized effort, political effort, to define the objectives that you would have—perhaps, in the vein of *I'll Take My Stand*—for a program aimed at the restoration of community. It's very difficult to convince a multinational corporation that somehow it should give up some of its power and resources and be taxed to support a movement away from the mass society, particularly the ghetto society. I think this is going to be forced upon the country in some sense, or there may be an apocalyptic breakdown. You know, these people don't surrender power easily. And I must confess that I'm a little bit vague now, as we were in the 1930s, about the political mechanisms, if this is to be a valid kind of movement.

I mention the fact that there's a growing interest in solar energy, which does provide a means for decentralization of power, and power then available to and adaptable to the small farmer, the individual. You can have gadgets, if you like. I see no harm in gadgets, if they are productive.

I would like to cite a remarkable piece that I read recently in the *Wall Street Journal*. I'm not a subscriber to the *Wall Street Journal*, although I must say it's one of the better informed newspapers in the country, and I buy it from the newsstand on a Friday, or sometime, just to keep up with what the enemy is up to. But this one *Wall Street Journal*, Tuesday, October 14, 1980: "Control Data" the headline says, "Control Data puts its computers to work helping farmers make it on small plots."

Now, the Control Data Corporation is one of the major competitors to IBM. They are not about to be interested—although some of the stockholders, I think, would disagree with that—in just giving money away on quixotic enterprises. But the chairman of the board of Control Data Corporation, which is a giant multinational computer organization, has a program which is called "Rural Venture." The idea is to adapt high technology to the needs of the individual small farmer. Now, Control Data is talking about the man with forty acres (or less) and a mule, and they have bought up in Minnesota a fair amount of land—I forget, several thousand acres, I think—on which they're experimenting in resettling individuals and groups and trying to help them to manage their affairs so as to make a living. They're not in it to subsidize small farmers, although this is being subsidized as a development.

I could hardly recover in time to eat dinner when I read about "Rural Venture." Maybe this is just a quixotic gesture, but a hard-headed chairman has persuaded his board to go along with him. I think the point is, if there really can be decentralization of energy, solar energy, so that you're not dependent on the mass industrial generation of power, as with the nuclear plant or even a hydroelectric plant—although that's better—that rural life could be made more attractive to, more feasible for, more productive for, the individual farmer.

I think in the connection of the black man who talked about wanting to get back home—he was perfectly willing to go back to his farm and his family and the community, and perhaps subsist there. We need to reconceive the means by which people could return to the land in a way which would not simply create the kind of dichotomy and opposition that we had to agrarianism in the 1930s: we want everybody to have forty acres and a mule and we want him to work from four o'clock in the morning to midnight with no rest in between, do all of the chores. This is not attractive, and probably isn't productive. But such a reconception will require a complete revision of national attitudes about social objectives, a whole new pattern of society, decentralization of a lot of industry. I don't mean the kind of decentralization which means that the mass industry in the Northeast and the Midwest is going to dash to the sunbelt in order to exploit the section more effectively—a new kind of carpetbagger coming down, many of them, Arabs for all I know—with resources to buy up the climate, the sunlight, and the other advantages. In that case we would be worse off than before.

I don't hold with Barry Commoner in all of his views. He has a lot of followers who seem a little bit queer to me, but he has said some very sensible things. Some of you may have read his *New Yorker* articles on the decentralization of electric power. I don't think he has thought through to our kind of idea. But I just throw that out in saying that, on the constructive side, there are now realistic possibilities that make the sorts of things we said in *I'll Take My Stand* seem more feasible.

Mr. Lytle: Let me ask you one question. There's nothing in there to control the weather, is there?

Mr. Lanier: No, you don't control the weather, but you try to control your behavior in the face of the weather. I'm not advocating this guy's machine, but it was an attitude that I thought was extremely unusual and possibly productive.

Mr. Lytle: Well, another thing that worries me about that black man coming down here, the community is shaking; it's not really there, maybe, but it's better than where he is.

Mr. Lanier: Better than where he is. He can go out of the house at night and feel safe—

Mr. Lytle: That's a sad kind of thing.

Mr. Lanier: —maybe.

Mr. Brooks: Red, would you like to take up that point, or take up something we ought to be talking about and have only glanced at and not dealt with at all?

Mr. Warren: It's been touched on in many ways. I recently read a book called *Connections*. This book was written by a man who gave a very famous series of BBC programs, some time back, on the nature of invention. The book is about technology: the real key inventions over the ages is what the programs were about. And the book is extraordinarily interesting to me. I recently spent a hitch among the men in white, and quite trivial a matter it was, but I had a radio or TV for the first time since I last was in the hospital for three days thirty years ago. They had a program—thing's going to be done in America, the same program called *Connections*, and the same man giving it—but it was rather different from the book—they did it a little differently. After they got through with the first key invention, the plow, they remarked how it made the city possible, provided extra food for the first time, and moved us away from tribal life. Well, they got through with the American version of it—maybe they did it first in the British Isles, but this was the American version, anyway—and then they called in a committee of scientists to comment on it, and doctor so-and-so of MIT and doctor so-and-so of this place, and Pasadena—they had four or five eminent scientists, all fine beards and piercing eyes, and held their chins like that (demonstrating). And they asked them what they thought. One man said: "Well, man made technology, he can control it. He can use it for his purposes." That's his argument: it's man-made, therefore man controls it. But does he? Henry Adams didn't think so. He said: "Does man ride the machine or the machine ride man?" That's one thing we do not know yet, does man run the machine or does the machine run man? We don't know.

Then they all agreed—not one of them raised the question: Does the machine have an effect on man? These wise men, you see, philosophers of science and men with strings of honorary degrees and all great names in this world of science, and not one asked this question: What is the effect of the world of technology on man? Yet the whole program was about that, but not one raised the question at all, which is the key question: Does it ride man? If so, how? The question did not occur to a one of these great thinkers, not one.

I just throw that in.

Mr. Brooks: Well, it's quite a load to throw in. This is a matter that has been discussed for a long time: What kind of truth does science give? Certainly it gives us truth, it gives a very important kind of truth. On the other hand, is it possible that science is highly limited in the kinds of truth it can provide? Mine isn't an anti-scientific statement, far from it. But if science is technician-in-chief to civilization, and the great master of technology and provider of means, isn't it just as important to know what the ends are and have some people thinking seriously, and talking seriously, about those ends? How do you establish values? Are they purely subjective? Is there any objective basis for them? I'd like to hear you speak to this, Mr. Lanier.

Mr. Lanier: Let me respond to an implication of something you had to say. I think one of the faiths that scientists, and lots of other people, had for a long time was that these problems that seemed to be generated by physical science and engineering technology, industrial organization, and development would ultimately be solved by the social sciences. The theory was that the social sciences lagged behind the physical sciences, but once they were built up to the point where there was sufficient understanding of the dynamics and the operation of societies, somehow, automatically, there would emerge means of social control of physical technology and development. I never shared this faith, really. I was never opposed to social science, having practiced it in a feeble way, part of it for a good part of my life, but I never had faith or any belief that the social sciences were going to provide direction, that is to say, to provide a set of values. They would tend to get off into the business of how to ameliorate conditions: if there is some social pathology here, then there are certain things you can do to poultice and patch things up. But what are the ends of existence? And can you mobilize and direct social science, or all science, in such a way that you will get guidance about what these ends ought to be, and guidance about the means for achieving the ends? I don't think so. I don't deprecate at all the idea that understanding should be cultivated; people should not remain just deliberately ignorant. If there is a possibility of understanding something, try to understand it. But part of understanding in this case is some awareness that this monster you have built up, in the way of national science and technology, has a character that removes it from the normal kinds of control that we have: individual or political. This makes it very difficult, indeed, regardless of what your values are, to say how you go about controlling this sort of power: economic power, social power, technological power, however you describe it.

A point I was trying to make here is that I think that present practices of industrialism and the uses of technology on the pattern of ever increasing productivity bear in themselves the seeds of their own destruction, because of the excessive use of energy and the depletion of nonrenewable resources. That destruction may destroy us all. The point is: What are the ends? What are the values? I think this is the kind of thing that *I'll Take My Stand* in 1930 was really trying to get at: humanistic sorts of living; various sorts of what we would call positive values.

But I'm also getting to one of Red's remarks, maybe it was Andrew, about the devil and the other pole. There is, in some sense, if you can be quasi-poetic about it, evil in man and good in man, and these forces of evil and good are ineradicable. They are not going to go away. The nuclear scientists developed nuclear fission, and all of the knowledge, and the machinery that came out of it, and what do we have as its most prominent use? Missiles, military hardware; secondarily, the generation of power which poisons things—they still don't know what to do with the residue, the nuclear wastes.

So I say that I'm not optimistic that decentralization and

movement in the direction of a neoagrarian kind of society are just naturally going to take place. But I think that the objective situation has changed somewhat favorably in that the nature of technology and science are more generally understood than they used to be. The problem is how, through political power, some means might be devised for controlling them.

Let me just mention one thing and then I'll stop. I think we have had plenty of illustrations of how power can be exercised politically through the environmentalist movement. These people influence votes. Now it's not a coherent movement. There are people who are nature lovers; they don't want to see a single bird species destroyed. There are other people who simply don't want to be poisoned; they are interested in health. But you can get these people all together, and believe me, congressmen listen to them.

Poor Mr. Commoner isn't going to get over 3 percent of the vote. He has some other ideas that don't commend him highly to voters, but with which I have some sympathy. Commoner wants to control the multinational corporations through some kind of nationalization of these sources of power. And I said in 1936 it seemed to me you have to move two ways. To get control of this kind of power you're going to have to have political power that is commensurate with it; in the other direction, this would facilitate decentralization of ownership and better distribution of the benefits of mass technology—assuming there are some. (And I think we would agree that these products are not necessarily all bad.) But that is a political problem. I think it's one of the main political problems facing this generation, and several other generations to come: how to come to terms with what seems to me the inevitable destruction of the planet if you just go on in the direction of ever-increasing growth of industrialization and corporate power. Reversing this direction would amount in some sense to "changing human nature"; that is, building up altruistic elements—building up what Freud would call "life instinct" and somehow moderating the "death instinct." Instead of God and the devil, and good and evil, Freud sort of polarized these forces this way. A lot of people find fault with that conceptual framework, but he was getting right at the point that in every man you have these conflicting sets of impulses, and the problem is what do you do about it? I'm sorry, the speech is too long!

Mr. Brooks: Not at all.

Mr. Warren: Just one thing I want to add to what Lyle was saying and to summarize what I was saying before: Man is not only economic man, that's not the only kind of man we have. We are economic humanoids. But we also are philosophical ones. The most ignorant, stupid man is a philosopher in his own way. He is bound to grope towards this or that, or some notion of what is true or not true. He can't survive otherwise, except in an institution being fed with a spoon. Also man is a value-making creature. That's even prior to being the philosophical man. He is a value-making animal, whether he knows it or not. He lives by values, more or less chosen by him and created by him. He is also the art-making animal, however deprived, degraded, or primitive, he is an art-making animal, whether he knows it or not. He is a myth-making animal—and we live by myths of one kind or another. All I want to say is that this question cannot be discussed except in those general terms, all those terms. You can't discuss the economic man without the philosophical man, or the philosophical man without the artistic man. They all imply value-creating processes that man inevitably is stuck with. So as far as man is not all of these he is not human. He has merely the shape of man but he is not human, he's not a complete man. And I'm not talking about so-called mental defectives at this point.

Mr. Brooks: I think one of the most remarkable confirmations and endorsements, in its own way, of *I'll Take My Stand* is a book which came out of the political left, two or three years ago. Some of you have read it, by Christopher Lasch, who is an important historian, very much interested in sociology and psychology. It's called *The Culture of Narcissism*. And the remarkable thing is to find agreement, essential and substantial agreement with the agrarians coming from that quarter. He is talking about the "me generation" and the erosion of community. Here is a man who says, very frankly, that religion, of course, is an illusion, but that the consequences of the weakening and the loss of religion in America have been bad and so on and so on in chapter after chapter—chapters on our mixed-up sexual mores; on whether people are happy or not, etc. Americans are perhaps better sexual technicians than ever before, but apparently their technical know-how isn't producing the joy which is widely advertised.

Now mind you, I don't know what Christopher Lasch would say if he has ever read *I'll Take My Stand*. He might be the last person in the world to want me to quote him as endorsing us. On the other hand, he is subscribing to point after point, though from a position on the other quarter. And what is his conclusion? What is his positive conclusion? It amounts pretty much to what you have heard the last few minutes. Let's hope, he seems to say, that there is enough common sense left—uncommon sense—shreds of community, willingness to see what's happening, that can be mobilized in America to counteract some of these destructive tendencies. In other words, he has no more *positive* recommendations in 1978 than were suggested in *I'll Take My Stand* in 1930.

Well, Lasch is an ally whom none of the three of you may want to accept any more than he might want to become your ally, and I accept his position with qualifications. But I think his book constitutes a very important kind of endorsement, and one that ought to be impressive to the person who says, "Oh, well, *I'll Take My Stand* is a book done by a bunch of poets; it's obsolete. The contributors wanted to go back to the plowing stick," and that kind of thing.

Brother Andrew, do you have a comment you would like to make?

Mr. Lytle: This is very brief. Red, I'd like to add to that: the family man, which is almost extinct.

Mr. Warren: I accept that.

Mr. Lytle: Think what we have lost now, and without this I don't think any of these other things are going to restore us to a stable condition. We have lost the distinction between what is public and what is private. The door no longer means anything. Anybody can enter it.

Just let me give you a brief account of a situation that happened with my grandfather's brother, who went after the Civil War to Florida on Lake Ware. (About two million other people moved out, after that war, trying to find this thing which had been lost.) He had this wonderful Lake Ware fishing place. He took a wagonload of fish into town and began to sell them and a great big burly fellow came up and bought some and thought he would close the trade, with a witticism. He said: "You're so little your wife will have to shake the sheets to find you." Of course, Uncle Frank jumped on him. And of course they fought and the man got him down, but Uncle Frank put his legs and arms around the man and pulled out his pocketknife and began to slash him up and down the back. And the man hollered out, "Somebody come take me off this little man."

Well, all right, that shows you that you still have to have that basic sense of yourself and of the dignity of yourself and your family. The big person doesn't always win.

Notes on Participants

Cleanth Brooks. Gray Professor of Rhetoric, Emeritus, Yale University; author of *William Faulkner: The Yoknapatawpha Country* and other works of criticism.

George Core. Editor of the *Sewanee Review;* author of *Southern Fiction Today* and other critical studies.

Robert B. Heilman. Professor of English, Emeritus, University of Washington; author of *The Ways of the World* and other works of criticism and social commentary.

Lyle Lanier. Executive Vice President and Provost Emeritus, University of Illinois; author of "A Critique of the Philosophy of Progress" in *I'll Take My Stand*.

Andrew Lytle. Novelist, memoirist, social commentator, and critic; author of "The Hind Tit" in *I'll Take My Stand*.

John Shelton Reed. Professor of sociology, University of North Carolina; author of *The Enduring South* and other sociological treatises.

Charles P. Roland. Alumni Distinguished Professor of History, University of Kentucky; author of *The Improbable Era* and other historical studies.

Louis D. Rubin, Jr. University Distinguished Professor of English, University of North Carolina; author of *The Wary Fugitives* and other works of criticism and fiction.

Lewis P. Simpson. Boyd Professor of English, Louisiana State University; author of *The Brazen Face of History* and other scholarly and critical studies.

Robert Penn Warren. Novelist, poet, critic, and commentator on southern culture; author of "The Briar Patch" in *I'll Take My Stand*.